Praise for *Holding On to Love After You've Lost a Baby*

The kind of relational stress that a couple goes through after losing a child can be ugly and plain violent. The pain is raw, the wounds are open, and loving each other through the tragedy can almost feel impossible. The words Candy and Dr. Chapman have written are incredibly compassionate and kind—you will find genuinely helpful advice, stories, and resources. I'm in awe of the beauty that has come from such a devastating loss, and I'm thankful to be a witness to the legacy of love on these pages and words.

JETTY RAE
Singer-songwriter

Losing a baby has been one of the most painful things that I have ever gone through. Candy's and Gary's book, *Holding On to Love After You've Lost a Baby*, brings comfort and encouragement to grieving parents and gives insight into what's most helpful for friends of the grieving parents. The pages are filled with hope from those who have walked through the valley of losing a child.

MICHELLE DUGGAR
Mother of 19 children here on earth and in loving memory of our 2 babies in heaven, Caleb and Jubilee

Losing a child is an unspeakable loss. Instead of holding your little one in your arms you have suddenly become part of a club no one would ever want to join. How do you navigate the pain? How does your marriage survive such grief? Candy has been there, and in this book she will tenderly walk you down a path to healing, hope, and love.

SHEILA WALSH
Author of *Praying Women* and *It's Okay Not to Be Okay*

As a pastor, I've walked many families through the process of grief. However, as a dad I had no idea how to face it for myself. It is hard to fathom, but my wife and I have gone through sixteen pregnancies in total, resulting in eight healthy children and eight waiting for us in heaven. Each time there was grief. Each time required facing fear. And each time God's miraculous love brought healing. As I turned the pages of *Holding On to Love After You've Lost a Baby*, I experienced the healing grace of the Lord. I highly recommend this book. Consider resourcing your church, counseling ministry, and mom's groups with copies of Holding on to Love after You've Lost a Baby to have on hand to gift to people grieving.

JAMEY VANGELDER
Senior Pastor of The House Church

As parents who have experienced the loss of two children, we wholeheartedly recommend reading *Holding On to Love After You've Lost a Baby*. It is a great resource for parents walking through child loss and for friends and family walking along with them. Holding on to love after you've lost a baby is difficult, and this book reminds you that you're not alone, you're seen, and that healing doesn't mean forgetting your precious child. Remembering always, our boys, Dobbs and Reed.

GENTRY AND HADLEY EDDINGS
Bereaved parents, pastor at Forest Hill Church

Grief speaks a language all its own and this book provides one of the most thoughtful and compassionate approaches to ministering to those who are grieving. *Holding On to Love After You've Lost a Baby* is a book you will pick up time after time as you walk with people through their darkest days and guide them to that Light at the end of the tunnel.

JENTEZEN FRANKLIN
Senior Pastor, Free Chapel, *New York Times* bestselling author

As a parent and grandparent myself, I know that the loss of a child is the parent's greatest fear. The force of this fear must be met with an even greater force of love to endure such tremendous loss. Candy McVicar's insightful story and Gary Chapman's wisdom are a perfect combination. The strategic blend these two bring is how we as couples, families, and communities increase the experience of healing love and chase away crippling fear. There are few resources that I have found to be this succinct and powerful for the person who grieves.

DANNY SILK
President of Loving on Purpose
Author of *Keep Your Love On* and *Unpunishable*

What an incredible book! This is a book that everyone needs to read, whether you have experienced loss or not. I have been inspired reading how Candy and Stephen selflessly give away what they learned through the trauma of stillbirth and miscarriage, which translates that many thousands are being helped in their journey too. This book is a wonderful and significant resource for grieving parents and a brilliant help for those who want to help family or friends who suffer loss. Read it and let it reach the depths of your heart, soul, mind, and body, because as you do, hope will begin to arise.

NANCY GOUDIE
Author, motivational speaker, founder of Spiritual Health Weekends, and cofounder of ngm and The Inspire Arts Trust

Holding On to Love After You've Lost a Baby is a gift to every parent who has experienced the worst kind of loss and the church leaders and friends called to come alongside. Having been on both sides of this dark valley, as a pastor and having lost our first child, Michael, in stillbirth, I can say from personal experience how valuable this book will be to the thousands of moms and dads silently grieving as well as those nearest to them who are searching for ways to love them through it.

RICH ROGERS
Director of Strategic Outreach and Editorial Director, Free Chapel

Candy and Gary have taken on an important and much-needed conversation with this book. I know first-hand the pain of losing multiple pregnancies to miscarriage; it can feel so difficult, isolating, and hopeless. Knowing how to navigate this journey with love will be a gift to so many.

MARIANNE RICHMOND
Bestselling author

What a refreshing truth to help bring healing to hurt! This is a book that should be read by every pastor, teacher, counselor, doctor, mother, and friend. Though I have raised 19 beautiful children, my heart still often feels the loss of our four miscarried babies that are in heaven. No one prepared me for the months of tears and the emptiness that I felt. Though amidst an army of loving family and friends, there was still a loneliness that gripped my heart. How I wish this book had been available those many years ago! What a joy and encouragement it has been to read it now. When the unthinkable happens—the loss of a child—our world turns upside down! Candy McVicar and Gary Chapman walk us through the challenges, the emotions, and even the relational issues that accompany this unexpected and devastating loss. Now there is hope for the hurting mom or dad, for the grieving friends and family who want to comfort but feel so helpless. I know this book will be a welcomed and treasured source of wisdom as you journey through this storm or as you help someone else through this painful road toward healing.

KELLY JO BATES
Mother to 4 precious babies in heaven and 19 wonderful children
Kelly, her husband Gil, and their family appear on the *Bringing Up Bates* reality TV show

HOLDING ON TO L♥VE AFTER YOU'VE LOST A BABY

The 5 Love Languages®
for Grieving Parents

GARY CHAPMAN, PhD
and CANDY McVICAR

Northfield Publishing

CHICAGO

Edited by Elizabeth Cody Newenhuyse
Interior and cover design: Erik M. Peterson
Cover texture copyright © 2018 by Charlie Waradee / Shutterstock (1199087374). All rights reserved.
Cover photo of footprints copyright © 2019 by Action Sports Photography / Shutterstock (56861266). All rights reserved.
Author photo of Gary Chapman © P.S.Photography
Author photo of Candy McVicar © Stephen McVicar

ISBN: 978-0-8024-1940-8

We hope you enjoy this book from Northfield Publishing. Our goal is to provide high-quality, thought-provoking books and products that connect truth to your real needs and challenges. For more information on other books and products that will help you with all your important relationships, go to northfieldpublishing.com or write to:

Northfield Publishing
820 N. LaSalle Boulevard
Chicago, IL 60610

1 3 5 7 9 10 8 6 4 2

Printed in the United States of America

To Grace and Promise, my babies in heaven. Though you were here on this earth ever so briefly, you impacted my life so profoundly. My love for you is everlasting. Until we embrace at our reunion . . . may your memory be a blessing. —Mom

Contents

About the Authors

GARY CHAPMAN is the author of the #1 bestselling 5 Love Languages® series and director of Marriage and Family Life Consultants. His books have been translated into more than fifty languages. Dr. Chapman travels the world presenting seminars and has appeared frequently on national media. He and his wife, Karolyn, live in North Carolina. They have a grown son and daughter and two grandchildren.

CANDY MCVICAR is a grief and trauma specialist who is on a mission to help couples and families grow closer together, heal, and cultivate new depths of love through their loss. Candy, with her beloved husband of twenty years, Stephen, is a mom to four—two on earth and two in heaven. In response to the stillbirth of their daughter Grace in 2001, they cofounded Missing GRACE Foundation to provide support, resources, and a place of healing for couples and families who have lost a baby or struggled with infertility or adoption challenges. Candy serves as the Executive Director. She is an author and gifted speaker who writes and delivers her messages with a candor and sincerity that connects her to those walking the journey of loss. She has been featured on Fox News, radio shows, and in numerous print and online publications. She also lectures across the nation at hospitals, universities, churches, and conferences. Visit www.candymcvicar.com. Candy and her family live in Hawai'i on the Garden Isle of Kaua'i, where they minister together at Aloha LIFE Church and the Abba's Robe Retreat for ministry leaders.

A Word from Gary

THROUGH THE YEARS, I have listened to the pain of parents who are grieving the death of their child. Whether they have experienced a miscarriage, stillbirth, SIDS, disease, or accident, the child they had anticipated is now dead. Physically, emotionally, mentally, and spiritually their world has been rocked. Things will never be the same.

How they process their pain, and how family and friends respond to the grieving couple will greatly impact their journey through grief. The deep sense of loss does not evaporate with the passing of time. The journey can be extremely lonely, especially when the couple has little or no support from others. Life must go on, but the physical and emotional pain makes it difficult to muster the energy to keep walking.

This book is written to grieving parents and their family and friends as a guide through the darkness. My coauthor is Candy McVicar. When I met Candy and heard her story I knew that she was the person with whom I wanted to write this book. She has walked through the valley of death in the loss of her firstborn, Grace, who was stillborn; and her fourth baby, Promise, whom she miscarried. Her journey was painful, and friends and medical personnel were not always helpful. However, in honoring Grace and Promise, Candy has left a legacy for others. In the last chapter of the book you will read of her journey and the ministry of the Missing GRACE Foundation.

Not only will you hear the empathetic voice of Candy but also the voices of scores of other grieving parents with whom she has walked for nearly twenty years. I was encouraged when I discovered that in her marriage and that of hundreds of grieving couples with whom she has worked, my book *The 5 Love Languages* helped them hold on to love while grieving the death of a child. Because moms and dads grieve differently, they often feel emotionally distant from each other. Learning to speak your spouse's primary love language can remove the distance and replace it with emotional intimacy. When the "love tank" is full, that is, when each of you feels genuinely loved by the other, the journey of grief is much more bearable.

At the end of each chapter you will find questions and suggestions that will help you process grief, individually and together. You will not read this book without tears, but I remind you that tears are an important part of healthy grieving. It is our desire that this book will help thousands of grieving parents, grandparents, siblings, extended family, and friends process their own grief and discover how to give constructive support to others who mourn. We believe it will be a significant resource for pastors, church leaders, counselors, social workers, nurses, funeral home directors, and other care providers to utilize as a guide for how to provide the most loving response and support to families when they experience a loss of a baby or a child. You also do not have to read the book straight through, but explore the sections that might be most helpful for your particular need. Again, we sincerely hope this book will be a valuable tool as you journey through grief and seek hope and insight.

—GARY D. CHAPMAN, PHD

1

When Your World Comes Crashing Down

News of your precious baby or child's death has launched
you into a terrifying unknown, and grief has parked its heavy
load on your heart. You are dismayed, lost, and heartbroken.
Now you must learn to survive and carry on, but how?

YOU WILL NEVER FORGET. You will always remember the moment—that life-altering moment in time when you heard those
stinging, dreaded words. "You better sit down . . . I am so sorry,
your child didn't make it." "There is no heartbeat." "We just
couldn't save your baby." "Your child was in an accident . . . the
injuries were too severe." "We found your daughter, but I am so
sorry, ma'am, she was murdered."

You heard the words, but they didn't make sense, they simply
didn't resonate. Did not compute. You looked at them in disbelief. Your brain searched for a way out of that surreal moment that
seemed like a cruel trick. Your mind tried in that flash of time to
escape the matrix, surely this was just a bad dream, you would wake
up and everything would be okay. But your mind was not playing

tricks on you: this was real, this was your real life playing out.

And this was a life just ended. Just like that, the child was here one moment and then instantly, there was no life in the body. No more breath in the lungs, no more pulse. The line on the monitor was flat. You didn't know it yet, but at that moment a piece of you died. Your baby, your child would no longer share in this life with you. Your world just came crashing down on you.

"NO! NO!!!!" you screamed aloud. Or maybe it just felt like you had screamed. You screamed in your soul while a silent cry escaped your mouth. You felt weak in the knees; your heart was racing, and tears spilled from your body as the truth set in. Sobbing ensued and piercing pangs of pain surged deep within your heart.

Maybe you didn't hear the news from someone else and you were the one who discovered that they were dead. You went to wake them from their nap and found your baby was cold and unresponsive. You went to the bathroom with back pain and contractions and your baby delivered far too early to have survived.

You would think that somehow after years of hearing of tragic stories in the news, viewing shocking stories in social media, seeing countless people die in movies, and reading terrifying horror stories of people's peril in the history of humankind, you would at least be a little prepared to deal with death. But nothing can prepare a parent for the death of their precious child. All those stories were not your story. They were someone else's, and though it may have moved you to feel compassion toward them, it didn't really affect you and your personal world. You know that bad things can happen to people, but not like this. Not to you. Not to a good person like you. Not to *your* baby, *your* son, *your* daughter. But something terrible and very sad did indeed happen, and now you must figure out how to survive.

HOW DO YOU "SURVIVE"?

What does "survive" mean? By definition it means to not die, to not disappear, to live through something and outlive someone else, to endure, to continue to exist, to carry on. When someone makes it through a horrible situation, they are called a survivor. Every parent who experiences the death of a baby or child can claim that title of "survivor" as they make passage through to the other side of the dark tunnel of grief to where there is light and hope again.

Once the (memorial) service is over, life around you can seem to speed on as normal, yet there is no return to life as it was in your home. As the reality sets in, the shock wears off and you will have to eventually find a new normal that incorporates your child who is very much alive in your mind and heart, while also very much absent in this physical world. You will need to learn how to live again and carry on in the land of the living. It may feel at times like the effects of grief could kill you because it hurts so badly, but the fact that you are reading this tells me you want to survive—and you will.

> You will have to find a new normal that incorporates your child who is very much alive in your mind and heart, while also very much absent in this physical world.

It's not uncommon to feel a need to escape, to want to disappear for a while. If it's a little trip to a distant land to get some rest and relaxation, then that kind of escape is good and can be very helpful. But if you run away thinking you can hide from and avoid dealing with the grief, it won't work. Grief will always find you and demand to be dealt with. Escaping for a day at a spa or to a decent movie is a perfectly healthy way to take a break from grief. Put it in a box on the shelf, and escape for a few hours. What isn't okay, though, is seeking relief through an often-harmful overabundance of spending, working, food, spirits, and drugs (prescription, over-the-counter, or otherwise).

You must "endure" life here without them. This literally means you suffer and tolerate disagreeable things. You are bearing a hardship. You didn't choose this for yourself. You didn't want this to happen, and the fact it did happen to you is very much disagreeable. It's OKAY to NOT BE OKAY with it.

Parents are not supposed to outlive their children. The order of this is not how it should have been. Truth is, none of this is how it should have been. You know you can't fix or change it but your mind will try. In your daydreams and in your sleep dreaming, your brain will perseverate with should-haves, could-haves, would-haves, what-ifs, and if-only thoughts. This is natural. It is trying to make sense of it, trying to figure out how to cope. It is trying to come to terms and accept the situation.

Notice in the definition of "survive" it says, "to continue to exist."[1] Initially, in the new, raw stages of grief, it will feel and look to others as if you're merely existing. You have a pulse, but on the bad days people close to you would be hard-pressed to find it. Simple tasks will prove to be laborious. The thought of having to get ready to leave for work can make you have a sense of panic and dread. As you anticipate all the steps it will take to get from A to Z for the morning—get out of bed, shower, shave, dry hair, get dressed, make coffee and breakfast, and drive to work—you may just give up and fall back into bed. Your mind, soul, and body are taxed to their limit. Grieving is hard work. It zaps all your energy and can put your drive in reverse or bring you to a standstill. In the grief world, we call this three steps forward and two steps back. You can make such good progress, only to find yourself seemingly back in the beginning stages of your grief.

ONE STEP FORWARD . . .

The process of grieving is not linear as some would hope, but rather it is a cyclical movement toward healing and peace. Meaning you won't typically get through a stage of grief or emotional point and pass through it, never to return to it again. You will come back through that same cycle of emotions and experience similar feelings again. However, the next time you are likely to be a little stronger and better equipped to handle the previous situation.

For example, think of the first time you went grocery shopping after your baby died. It was all you could do to remember the few things on your list—bread, milk, cereal, fruit, eggs, toilet paper, and tissues. In a daze, as you aimlessly pushed your cart through the store, you accidentally went too close to the aisle with the baby items, noticed the diapers and started to cry. Then when you got to the checkout lane, a new mom pulled in behind you to check out in your same line. She had her new baby tucked in in the car seat in the shopping cart. You overhear the next person in line say, "Oh, how adorable! What a sweet baby. How old is she?" "A week old," the mother replied. You felt like someone squeezed the air right out of your lungs as you panicked and nervously abandoned your cart, leaving the store in defeat without your groceries. I actually did this very thing a week after my baby died. I came home and when I walked in the door empty-handed, my husband, surprised, asked, "What happened to the groceries?" I just fell into a heap in his arms and bawled.

The next time you went grocery shopping, you remembered to avoid the baby aisle. But as you passed it, your heart quickened, tears filled your eyes, and a lump developed in your throat. It was still a very emotional and difficult task, but you left the store with a bag of groceries and felt a small bit of encouragement in achieving this small victory. By the tenth time you entered the grocery store, you did your shopping without too much difficulty and didn't even cry.

Remember, though, this is a not a linear healing process. Fast-forward to a year later, you are back at the store, and you spot the cutest baby item on display and you totally fall apart and feel wrecked. You wonder to yourself how a year later you can be such a mess when you had made such good progress. Then it dawns on you: your baby would be a year old, and that day at the store, you feel like you are back at square one emotionally. You miss her like crazy and the deep hurt is still there.

Sometimes it can also go in reverse—you get worse before you get better. For example, this can be true in situations where close friends or family have a baby or child who is close in age to the little one you lost. You had anticipated the kids growing up together, sharing many experiences and making special memories over the years. Now the relationship is strained, and you are sad every time you see and hear about their child. It gets harder each time you interact with them, so you end up avoiding them at all costs. You start to get angry and have dark feelings of jealousy that make you feel bad about yourself. "Why can't I just accept and love their child? It's not like I want something to happen to their child, but I just can't be around them without getting upset. They have theirs and I don't have mine. It's not fair."

Eventually, this relationship could grow distant until they are no longer in your life—that is, unless you determine to work through all those feelings, and you communicate honestly with your friend about the emotional challenge you are having. If they are a loving and patient friend, and you do the work of getting stronger and more at peace with the situation, you might actually find their child to be quite special in your life, and truly enjoy being around them. Even though it can be bittersweet at times, you are happier with them in your life than without them.

Additional definitions of "survivor" include: someone overcoming a traumatic experience, and "a person with great powers of endurance . . . somebody who shows a great will to live or a great determination to overcome difficulties".[2]

FEAR AND ANXIETY: THE EVIL TWINS

What exactly must a survivor overcome? The biggest hurdles are fear and anxiety, which can easily stop parents in their tracks when trying to make headway. Fear and anxiety often go hand in hand like two shady-looking strangers that you notice creeping around outside your house. They always seem to be lurking close by. It can feel like they follow you as closely as your own shadow in the early days and months of sorrowing. After experiencing a loss, you feel so vulnerable, and questions plague your mind of what other terrible things could also happen. You wonder how you can make it without your child. Fear and anxiety seem to whisper of more ill fate and doom. Don't entertain them. You must choose to give them walking papers. Put up a "No Trespassing" sign. If you should find that you can't manage in healthy ways in your grieving because their voices grow too strong, then it's time to get some help with a counselor, pastor, or doctor who can provide assistance.

Painful emotions can be alleviated and healed through expressing your feelings. Some excellent ways to do this are to: share them with a trusted loved one/friend, talk about them to God, meditate, breathe deeply, journal, exercise, find a creative outlet, turn on some soothing music, adopt an animal in need of a home that will bring comfort and life into your world, go and serve someone else in need, and open your life up to others.

Deep sorrow can feel like a long, dark night that shows no promise of a dawn. There's a thick low fog covering the surface of your heart and the sun can't seem to break through. "Weeping may endure for a night, but joy comes in the morning."[3] Joy comes in all shapes and sizes and looks different to everyone, but it will attempt to shine into your life each day. It is that ray of sun that pierces the dark cloud covering your heart. Don't miss it. It can be a butterfly, or a bird that lands close to you and you know it is there just for you. It can be the smile of a kind person who did a sweet gesture to lighten your load.

> No matter how short or long a time your baby or child lived, they mattered.

It can be simple text or letter with a few words of encouragement right when you needed to hear just those words. It can be the rainbow above, the white snowflakes on your eyelashes, the dolphin that jumps out of the water and you are sure it is smiling at you.

Just be open to the ways it will come to you. These joy blessings can come in disguise, so watch out for them.

No matter how short or long a time your baby or child lived, they mattered. Your child was significant and made an impact. What made him so special? That he was yours? Yes, that is one thing indeed that made him special. How would you complete this sentence? "My baby or child was special to me because_____."

It's the love you shared with each other that is most special. The greatest concern for bereaved parents is that their child will be forgotten—that soon, no one will care enough to remember. For the miscarried or stillborn baby, it's that no one even got to know the baby. So to others it seems the child never existed. Sadly, some people will forget and some will move on, and that is a hard fact to come to terms with. BUT your baby or child's story isn't over because you aren't finished here on earth yet, and the child lives on through you. Your tears are not wasted; nor do we believe that your hurt is wasted. Something good, something worth surviving for is in your future. That "something" is connected in a special way to your baby or child. It may begin with you sharing your story, or with you helping someone else as a way to honor your child's memory. Do what you can in your life to preserve their memory by sharing with others the love you have for your child.

There is a saying that "time heals all wounds," but don't buy it for a second. Time doesn't heal! It certainly takes time to learn healthy ways to cope and to take steps that bring forward motion in life. But time didn't do it for you. YOU do it step-by-step, one choice at a time. Be proud of yourself and celebrate the small victories. Though it may be three steps forward and two steps back in the early stages of grief, it is still progress.

YOUR TURN

- Can you recall any "joy blessings" that have come to you recently?

- What are some small victories you have achieved?

2

Grieving the Loss of
a Baby You Never Knew

In the wake of a pregnancy loss or the death of an infant,
parents feel brokenhearted. The loss of a baby you never knew
in this world is especially wrenching. Suddenly, the baby is
gone. There are few, if any, memories of your child. Without
even those memories for comfort, a deep, dark grief can
envelop the parents. Whether the loss occurred by an act of
nature, by an accident, by the choice of the parents, or by
someone who took the child's life, parents need support and
help in finding healthy ways to cope and heal.

LIKE WATCHING WATER while waiting for it to boil, it feels like
forever when you're waiting to read the results of a home pregnancy test. As a woman waits with anticipation in the bathroom,
she feels a surge of exhilaration and hope as she observes the second line appear that indicates she is positively pregnant. For some
women the news is confirmed after she's had her blood drawn for
hCG levels and the clinic calls with *the* news: "Yes, Mrs. Johnson,
the tests came back. Your numbers are doubling and it looks like

you are pregnant!" The next memory is often the moment she shared the news with her spouse or friend and it all became that much more real. How exciting to confirm that LIFE is growing inside her! A future ballerina, firefighter, president, doctor, the next generation to take on the family business—developing in her womb day by day. The outcome is sure: There will be a baby, a precious baby to cradle and to love.

The excitement and expectation is often married with a touch of anxiety and unending questions that race through her mind. Even though the due date is far off, the new mom will conjure up images of the nursery room completed, the full-bellied pregnancy clothes, the baby showers, and the birthing room.

The dad will have his own heightened mix of emotions as he contemplates his responsibility for his child's future and how he will provide for his baby. He will think of ways to bond with his child and how life will change as his family grows. He will look at his wife with pride as he gently touches her belly and imagines his son or daughter growing and developing each day.

The notion of the pregnancy ending prematurely is usually not on the radar for newly expecting parents. They are called "newly expecting parents" for a reason—they **expect** to bring home a baby, and they feel a sense of confidence that everything will work out okay. The window of time from finding out they are pregnant to the initial hours, days, and weeks of celebrating the new life growing within, is as tender and sweet as their "I Dos" at the altar. Innocently unaware, many newly expecting parents are free to blissfully go through pregnancy without an inkling of the risks of pregnancy loss. In fact, even though parents commonly read several books about pregnancy to prepare for the baby to arrive, rarely will the first time parents read the sections in the pregnancy books about the "bad or sad" things that can happen in pregnancy. They will avoid that information as they fear that knowing about the risk factors and challenging issues that can happen in pregnancy might make them worry more. Some may even go so far as to believe the falsehood that reading those things will somehow "jinx" their pregnancy to turn out badly.

THE COMPLEX EMOTIONS OF PREGNANCY

For couples who have been exposed to the heartbreak of a pregnancy or infant loss, either through hearing about it, watching a friend or loved one go through it, or personally experiencing a previous loss of their own, they will progress in the pregnancy with a little more reserve and heightened awareness of just how delicate life is. This knowledge affects couples differently. Some parents will bond more readily to their baby, investing more energy early on to express their love

> "Precious baby of mine, I will love you with all my heart for as long as I have the opportunity to share in your life."

for this new baby by singing, reading, talking, and praying for them. They will place their hands where they imagine the baby growing, and lovingly caress them. These actions are outward expressions of love for their baby, and a choice to love—no matter the outcome.

"Precious baby of mine. I will love you with all my heart for as long as I have the opportunity to share in your life. Hopefully my love will carry you through to the safety of my arms when it's your time to be born. If for some reason you don't make it safely, I will not look back with regret for having restrained my love for you. I will find comfort in the fact that you hopefully felt and knew of my love while you were being formed."

These were the words spoken to my belly and quietly in my heart to the daughter we affectionately called our "Rainbow Baby" (which bereaved parents call the baby in their subsequent pregnancy following a loss). We had a different perspective this time, and, as a couple, we agreed that this baby, our second child, would know early on of our love. As soon as we knew we were having another girl we named her and spoke to her by name. Every chance her daddy could be at a doctor's appointment and see his daughter on the ultrasound, he came and shared in the pregnancy journey as a way to bond with his daughter.

Some parents will wait to bond and will make a conscious or even unconscious choice to hold their hearts at bay until their baby is born. This is driven by a fear that loving their baby openly early on will just result in a deeper hurt if it doesn't work out and their baby doesn't make it into the world healthy and screaming. These parents may also find it is difficult to fully enter the joy and excitement of the pregnancy, but may later regret not expressing love for their baby sooner.

There are circumstances in which there are the "oops," and couples who aren't planning for or expecting to conceive find themselves pregnant. The surprise news forces them to evaluate how they feel about having a baby, and they may feel unsure if they want to follow through with the pregnancy. Initially, there may be discussions in which they express these feelings to one another with concern or in heated conversations. "I wasn't ready, we don't have the money right now, and we aren't even married yet. How are we going to do this?"

After the initial shock wears off, their worry turns to excitement, and the couple will embrace the idea of a baby (or babies if there are multiples) and prepare accordingly. Fears will fade to wonder, and wonder will turn to enthusiasm. Then after starting to get used to the idea, it can feel like a cruel trick if the pregnancy suddenly ends in a miscarriage or stillbirth. Guilty feelings can easily rise up within the parents. Words of blame can be hurled at each other: "You were the one who didn't want this baby; now look what happened. This is your doing!" Logically, they know their words didn't cause the baby to die, but as they cast about for answers to "why it happened," parents can internalize that lie.

A FATAL AND FINAL DECISION

Sometimes the death of a baby is intentional.

According to the Guttmacher Institute, choosing to end the pregnancy was an option performed approximately 862,320 times in 2017 in the USA[1] and between 2010–2014, they estimated that approximately 56 million induced abortions occurred each year worldwide.[2]

There are many factors that contribute to this fatal and final decision (age, incest, rape, casual relations, health of mom or baby, financial concerns, and the list goes on).

Though we view all life as precious and believe personally we should protect any life that is in danger of being cut short, we don't believe we should place judgment on anyone who has chosen differently in their past. Only love and grace should be extended toward the parents who chose otherwise. We have not walked even a mile in their shoes. Placing judgment and shaming someone only adds to their hurt and will never lead to a path of healing.

I (Candy) remember vividly the labor room experience of Lisa, who was delivering her son, who had a condition not compatible with life and would die shortly after birth. I was there to take photos and video of her baby to have as keepsakes and to help her create lasting memories once her baby was born. I was sitting at her bedside holding her hand as she began sobbing, grieving for the first time about an elective abortion she had undergone years prior. "I never got pictures of that baby, never held that baby, and I ended my own baby's life! I was young and so naïve, and I believed the nurse who told me my baby wouldn't feel anything, and it was no big thing . . . I will never forgive myself . . . how could I have done that to my baby? Oh GOD . . . please forgive me, I am so sorry!" Then she asked me, her face puffy and tearstained with mascara lines down to her chin, if this baby of hers, that she wanted so badly, was being taken from her by God because she had taken the life of her other baby through an abortion. She was just realizing the full weight of her decision years before; and now this baby's birth made the emotions and memories of her abortion come front and center in her mind, straight from the place she kept them hidden within the closet of her heart.

I shook my head "no" as I hugged her and cried with her, consoling her as best I could. He's not like that. She knew my words were sincere and that I was hurting with her as I entered the pain of her story. I shared a verse that had comforted me in dark times, "Peace I leave with you; my peace I give to you. Not as the world gives do I give to you. Let not your hearts be troubled, neither let them be afraid."[3] In that moment she accepted in faith the forgiveness and peace she had needed. We both felt the darkness and weight lift from her chest and from the room, and shortly afterward she delivered and held her baby boy. Though she stated she had a hole in her heart, she said she no longer felt shame and fear. She was smiling as she expressed how grateful she was to meet and hold her precious baby, and what a blessing it was to have pictures with her son. She kissed him over and over and cradled him close and sang to him. It was a beautiful and sacred moment in time.

When a baby's life is cut short, whether by an act of nature or by personal choice, it hurts the mother at her core. Fathers hurt too, and the decision for them is also difficult, but the mother is the one who must physically submit her body to the act of termination. Whether the baby was "wanted" or not, if she chooses to abort and end her baby's life, eventually grief will stand at the door of her heart demanding to be addressed.

Fathers feel a deep weight in their souls. Did he persuade the decision, did he have no say, or did he express a lack of interest or enthusiasm for the pregnancy? His actions can make all the difference in his partner's decision to carry to term or not—and he knows he is responsible for his part of what got them into this in the first place. It is a helpless feeling not to be able to save his baby if his partner carries out an abortion without his knowledge or even after he tried to convince her to keep the baby.

The pain of grief in a daddy's chest intertwines like a thorny vine around the layers of his tender heart as he contemplates what kind of legacy and heritage was lost. After crying or raging and not knowing what to do with all the unfamiliar emotions, he tells himself to buck up, get over it, and move on. His friends echo his internal dialogue reaffirming he is on the right track of thinking. He is offered a beer for comfort, and he lets his mind focus on the TV or the hobby that keeps him busy so he can keep the thoughts at bay. Though the thorns remain, he mentally chooses to harden his heart at that moment to avoid feeling any more pain. Outwardly, he seems fine. But the meteorologist would say the forecast shows he's partly cloudy with a likelihood of severe thunderstorms throughout the night.

"I WANT TO TALK ABOUT THEM"

Baby-making is serious business. The consummate act of two becoming one flesh is taken far too lightly in our world today. Casual encounters are sadly common, and the ramifications of sex are discarded afterthoughts. Making a baby is a most profound and holy act. For a female, having the ability to experience this rite of passage, to co-labor with God in the ultimate expression of love that we call procreation and physically partake in the miracle of conception to make another human in the image of God and then to grow internally, deliver, and grow externally at the breast this new human life—to participate with God in nurturing this new life is a most high honor.

If the process of growing this baby internally, or after birth externally, is interrupted and the life is cut short, the mother feels incomplete, like a part of her is cut off. Her mother's heart will forever bear the scar.

Marge's story includes two such deep scars on her heart. I (Candy) will never forget the amazing story she shared with me at the end of a conference I had organized for families who had experienced a pregnancy or infant loss. She approached me at the door as I was saying goodbye to our guests. "Hi, you don't know me and before a few weeks ago when I heard you on the radio, I didn't know about you either, but I knew I had to come and meet you. My name is Marge, and I want to thank you. You see these two candles I am holding. I want to tell you about them."

The candles she was referring to had been set out on a commemoration table. Parents were invited to light one in memory of every baby they have in heaven and then at the end of the night they were to take their candles home as a keepsake. As I looked into her tear-filled eyes, I couldn't help but notice the deep grooves of lines life had etched in her face.

Marge continued. "When I heard you tell your story on the radio, I was driving on a country road and I started crying so hard I couldn't even see to drive, so I pulled over until I finished crying. When I got home, I found my husband in his usual place at the kitchen table watching TV with a drink in his hand. I made a matter-of-fact announcement, knowing he could hear me. 'I want to talk about them, Fred. People talk about their babies now, they see and hold them, and they go to support groups. I want to know about my babies. I have to find out something. I NEED to know something about our babies.'

"My husband didn't respond to my comments; he simply set down his drink, got up and grabbed the keys and said, 'Let's go.' I was infuriated. 'No!' I yelled, 'I am no longer going to live like this. I can't take it anymore! I am serious. It's time; I want to talk about our babies—NOW! You can't just push it back under the rug and ignore it anymore.' He explained to me that he only knew of one way to help me, and it required that I get in the car and go somewhere with him. Upset and confused, I complied and got in the car crying.

"You see," she said, "these two candles represent my first two children. Over forty years ago we went through two different full-term pregnancies that ended in stillbirths. I never got to see my babies, never got to hold them, and I didn't even get to find out their genders. I had to leave the hospital without my babies after their births and was expected to just 'forget about it' and was told to go home and gather myself and then try for another.

"We have lived in the same little town of a few hundred people all these years and driven past the same cemetery on our drive to and from town . . . now we were turning into the cemetery. We pulled up and there before me were two grave markers with names and dates. I stared in disbelief at the dates and though the names were unfamiliar to me, the dates were burned into my memory. These were the graves of MY BABIES! I screamed and wailed and fell to the ground clutching the grass, and waves of emotion flooded my body. I was now keenly aware that they existed and they weren't a figment of my imagination; they had names and I could finally learn if they were boys or girls. But I was confused and shocked. How did my babies get here and get names and why had I not been told?

> "Healing began for both of us as I slowly began to learn about my babies."

"My husband was weeping beside me on his knees and for the next hour he told me everything, and a huge weight was lifted off his shoulders. Healing began for both of us as I slowly began to learn about my babies. You see, back then things were different; we didn't get to see or hold our stillborn babies. My husband respectfully but firmly had requested that the doctor let him take our babies so they could have a proper burial. The doctor spoke words that terrified my husband. 'Under one condition will I let you take them. Your wife must never find out. If you want her to spend her life in a straitjacket in a mental institution, then tell her, but I know for a fact that women aren't strong enough to handle these things and you will only hurt her if you let her see or find out about the baby. We know it is better for them if we just all forget about it and move on.'

"My husband held high regard for our doctor and the doctor's word was gospel back then. They had their private handshake and agreement, and Fred was obedient to comply with the doctor and he never spoke a word of it to me. But he named the babies and buried them. And over time his trust and faith in this doctor eroded. He saw that hiding it from me, and my not knowing anything, had made me crazy anyway. I became an agoraphobic and an addict. Refusing to talk about it with me made us drift apart and we just stopped talking. We were just miserable roommates. He told me that he had been visiting them regularly at the cemetery, and he felt so guilty for knowing them when I didn't. But the lie was so big he could never bring himself to tell me. So he was actually relieved when I came home and told him I wanted to talk about it. Thank you, Candy, because of you, I have 'met' my babies finally, and I feel alive for the first time in forty years. I can't tell you how amazing it is to know about them and to call them by name, and be able to visit them. Healing and restoration are happening in my life and my marriage. Thank you for sharing your story."

I gave her a big bear hug and tears dripped from my face onto her shoulder as I thanked her for sharing her story with me. As I watched her walk down the hallway, I sensed our interaction was affecting and defining my life's work. I resolved in that moment to do what I could in life to validate the significance of each baby that dies, to affirm the fact that parents absolutely need support when they suffer the loss of a child (which includes ongoing acknowledgment that their baby is not forgotten), and that each person has a right to their own unique grief.

31

We fool ourselves if we think that baby-making is no big deal. If we flippantly respond to what happens to these little lives as if they are not significant, we join the masses in the world that tout an overriding message to "get over" any baby that dies. As if it were a breakup of a bad relationship, and we are now better off and can move on, putting that all behind us. Parents aren't wired to forget and not care. That's why it doesn't work well when we *try* not to care. We can't pretend it didn't happen. Each baby matters and is missed on earth and has an eternal spirit in heaven.

Historically, parents like Marge and Fred seldom were given the opportunity to see or hold their baby. Babies that had died or were expected to die shortly after birth were usually whisked away by the hospital nurse and parents were told, "It is for the best that you not see the baby, and you should try to just move on with your lives and try for another when you're ready." Even today, this antiquated way of thinking can overshadow the mounting research proving the benefits and improved outcomes for parents who hold and create memories with their baby. It is normal for parents to feel scared to hold their dead or dying baby due to fears of seeing a baby with physical changes or deformities. It is normal for parents to fear that if they don't dissociate early on it will only hurt worse when they have to say their goodbyes. But this is a false notion. There are no do-overs when delivering a baby that has died or won't survive very long. Each decision the parents make is a final one, and parents have to live with the consequences of that decision. Parents who don't get the chance to see and hold their baby indeed struggle with this later on and find they aren't coping well with their regrets.

THERAPY FOR DEEP WOUNDS

Today there are a variety of effective therapies and methods that can be used to help heal from traumatic memories, regrets, and deep emotional wounds such as those suffered by Marge and Fred. I have heard encouraging testimonies from bereaved parents who shared with me how helpful it was for them to work with an EMDR specialist (Eye Movement Desensitization Reprocessing)[4] or a Brain Spotting specialist.[5] Both of these utilize the observation of eye movement in the session to address the trauma and find where the person is "stuck." There are also excellent expressive, interactive, and integrative mental health therapies to consider: Sand Tray, Sand Play,[6] Art,[7] Music,[8] and Equine-Assisted therapy.[9] Each of these is especially beneficial for children and adolescents dealing with trauma, grief, and depression, and work beautifully for adults too.

Personally, I (Candy) found inner healing through pastoral prayer ministry. I was so impressed by the breakthrough I experienced to release the trauma, pain, and emotional wounds, I went through training so I can now help offer inner-healing prayer ministry for others. It is a way to invite God into your pain and memories and to pray through each one and accept His love and healing touch in each of those memories.

NO BABY TO HOLD

There will not be a baby to hold at birth if they are diagnosed as having a molar pregnancy or ectopic pregnancy. In molar pregnancies, there are extra chromosomes, and the fertilized egg (embryo) and placenta develop abnormally. Or there is no embryo, and the placenta develops abnormally. An ectopic pregnancy happens when the egg becomes fertilized, however, it begins to grow outside of the uterus in either the fallopian tube or the abdomen. Most babies are not able to thrive with this circumstance. In both molar and ectopic pregnancies, the medical options are not what any mom wants to face. Both are difficult choices of either strong medications and/or surgical removal and add to the heartbreak of the loss.

If there is an early miscarriage, which is up to thirteen weeks gestation in the first trimester, there is the possibility to deliver the baby fully and to see the tiny baby. They can be as small as a bean or cashew nut and could fit into the palm of an adult hand. The earlier on it is or the longer the baby has been in utero but has already passed, the more likely the baby will be too small to hold or even see.

Molar, ectopic, and miscarried babies may be delivered at a hospital with a medical procedure called a "D&C," which means dilation and curettage, and is often necessary to complete the removal of the baby and associated tissue from the pregnancy if the mother is not able to naturally deliver everything safely. The baby may also miscarry in the toilet, and to the mother's horror and dismay, she may have accidentally flushed, not realizing the baby had been expelled while she sat on the toilet. The baby may not be recognizable as a baby if miscarried before twelve weeks, even if she is able to collect and contain what comes forth through her laboring. The evidence that the baby really was "here," and truly did exist, may only be in the form of the pregnancy test or, at best, the ultrasound picture. This is added pain for the parents.

The parents who miscarry may or may not have told anyone they were even pregnant. The mother might go back to work the next day after her miscarriage without anyone even knowing the turmoil she is experiencing. All around her, there are pregnant women, babies in car seats and strollers, and news of pregnancy announcements. She suffers alone in silence. What is typically the first question a woman is asked? "So, do you have any children?" How is she to respond? "Yes, but I just miscarried." And then she must deal with the person's responses, which she is not prepared to handle, especially if the comments are unkind. Or should she say, "No, I don't have any kids," (and then feel terrible because she is denying the fact she does have a baby but it died). If she simply says "yes," she knows there will be further questions to answer like, "Oh, how many, what ages, boy or girl?" For a man, what is the common first question he is asked in a casual conversation? "So, what do you do (for a living)?" He can usually avoid the kid questions a little easier if he wants to steer clear. The question about children is usually much further down the line of questions, but when he encounters the question, the pain tugs at his heart whether he chooses to be open about the loss of his baby or not. It is a difficult road to navigate the questions "Do you have children" and "How many do you have?" For the bereaved parents, this will always be tricky and feel like a sting to their heart when they answer.

FINDING HOPE

Life, at its earliest point recognized at conception, is precious, and each baby is a miracle and a treasure. The progression of who that baby will become may not be realized on earth, but we believe it will be realized in heaven, and you will see them again and know them fully. "We do not want you to be uninformed, brothers, about those who are asleep, that you may not grieve as others do who have no hope."[10] When you have faith in God, you can grieve with hope. You can be confident that your baby is in heaven, and you will be with them again. If you do not have faith in the existence of God, Jesus' redemptive death on the cross that paid the penalty for our sins, or heaven, please consider taking the leap from unbelief to belief. We have faith in so many things without having the ability to test them, without knowing exactly how they came to be, and even without having firsthand experience with them ourselves.

You have faith in some things. I am guessing you trust that the sun will be there every morning and the moon there every night. This book you are reading—did it form by itself? Did the words one day merge together and create sentences and punctuation and then chapters? Did the pages gravitate to pull together inside a cover that held and protected the pages within? Or were there authors who created this book? There is a Creator who formed the heavens and the earth and created you and your baby!

YOUR TURN

1. Get two sheets of white paper and draw an outline of a gingerbread man on each sheet of paper. Now take some time to think about how your grief feels in your body. Color inside the body of the gingerbread man with different colors that describe the way your emotions feel. For example, at one point in my grief journey, I might have colored mine with a grey gloominess shadowing the mind on the head of the gingerbread figure, and colored red on the chest for the fire and heat that was in my heart from anger, and colored dark

blue over my arms as that represented the achy feeling of longing I had. Put the date at the top and a title: "What my grief looks like today."

2. Now with the second gingerbread man outline, go somewhere in your mind where you feel loved, you feel peaceful, safe, and comforted. Then draw what that feels like. For example, I would go to the ocean and float in the sea and ride the waves. My gingerbread figure would have yellow over my mind, hands, and feet where the sun gave warmth, and a light sky-blue color over my chest where I felt a sense of well-being. Put the date at the top and a title: "What my grief can look like today."

This exercise helps you to identify how your emotions are affecting your physical body. You can imagine yourself going to the peaceful place with your second drawing when the emotions are too intense and difficult to navigate.

3. What are some ways you can share about your baby and show love for your baby with others?

3

Our Journey

I invite you to enter into my story of grief. I share these intimate details in hopes it proves helpful in some way and will encourage you to share your story. For it is in sharing your baby's story that your healing begins and their life is acknowledged and they continue to make an impact.

MY HEART WAS EAGER with anticipation for the day I would get to share in the beautiful title of being called a "mom." I was thrilled to share in this amazing rite of passage as a woman. After having been married over a year, we felt ready to try to conceive. We figured we would start early. Friends in our close circle had experienced infertility, so we were mentally prepared for the possibility that it might take some time to get that positive pregnancy test. Contributing to our concern was that my husband, Stephen, had undergone several heart surgeries in his early twenties, and it was feared that the long exposure to radiation for the images taken during the surgeries might cause some fertility issues. We hoped to have children of our own but also considered adoption, and we talked about being foster parents. We knew that we would have children in our home, no matter the path they took to join our family. To our delight and surprise, the first try was a success. At the time, we thought that if we made it through the first trimester without miscarrying, the baby was safe and our good outcome secured.

I knew of other women who had miscarried, so I was a little reserved in expressing too much outward enthusiasm for the pregnancy. I was very concerned about the possibility of a miscarriage due to the spotting I had experienced. I said quietly to myself and to God, "Please don't let me lose this baby, but if I have to for some reason, let it be now and not later." I unknowingly thought the heartbreak of loss would be much easier to deal with if I lost the baby early in the pregnancy. The reality, however, is that I loved this first baby of ours from the moment we found out we were expecting. My heart was connected as soon as I had the sensation that I was likely pregnant.

A PAINFUL PREGNANCY

We were thrilled to be expecting our first child. This was to be the first grandchild on my side and the second on Stephen's. I wish I could say that the joy continued through the pregnancy, but from the start, it was fraught with challenges and pain. I had severe hyperemesis (extreme vomiting) for six months and was at the mercy of the nearest bathroom or Ziploc baggie no fewer than ten times a day. This created a domino effect of other problems, including disabling back pain, a loss of

> I would have endured far greater pain if I knew it could have saved her.

more than twenty pounds, and severe dehydration. I ended up having bronchitis and then pneumonia. The antibiotics wreaked their own havoc as well. To say I was miserable was an understatement, though in retrospect, it was hardly misery compared to how I would feel after my daughter was born lifeless. I would have endured far greater pain and suffered longer if I knew it could have saved her.

From thirty weeks into the pregnancy, I felt less and less movement. I only felt her move mildly five to ten times a day. She had never been very active but was especially quiet those last few weeks. Seven times I called the doctor, hoping they could find out what was wrong and help us, and each time was told to drink orange juice and lie on my side. "Try eating some M&Ms," the nurse recommended over the phone. I tried, but nothing changed. Their thought was that my sugar intake would get the baby moving, which would assure me that she was okay. They never mentioned or provided kick count information. Had they, it would have explained that babies in the third trimester should have some kind of movement (taps, kicks, rolls, flutters) an average of ten times every two hours[1]—without the added stimulation of sugar in the blood.

I went to the clinic often, asking for testing to find out what might be wrong. I was only offered a Doppler check for fetal heart tones. They would find a satisfactory heart rate eventually after several attempts. I was ushered out with a pat on the back and comments to the effect of, "Stop being a worrywart—you and your baby are just fine. You have a while yet to go."

On the seventh visit I made to the clinic, they finally sent me for the ultrasound I had been requesting all along. I am forever grateful for the fact that my husband was able to get out of work to come to the appointment with me. As the radiologist told us the news that altered the course of our life forever, she presented the information devoid of any kindness, mercy, or respect: "There's NO heartbeat. 'It' is dead. You must now go to the hospital to take care of 'it.'" As cold as that sounds, that was exactly how icily those words were spoken to us.

It got worse. She instructed us to leave the building out the back door, because I was crying, and she didn't want me to upset the pregnant new moms in the waiting room. The treatment and the words spoken were shocking, but we were too stunned to do much about it.

The next morning, labor was induced at the hospital. I began the scary and unfamiliar experience of labor, all the while wondering if some miracle would occur, changing the outcome to a live birth. We held out hope that they had misdiagnosed the situation. Perhaps we could leave with our baby rather than departing with empty arms and no baby in the car seat.

AT THE HOSPITAL

We were a day shy of thirty-three weeks gestation and had not completed our birthing classes, so we were both uncertain how to do labor and delivery. In the earlier stages, we walked the halls, trying to keep our minds on lighter things. We even joked some and laughed a bit as we tried to distance ourselves from our reality. As the hours dragged on and the pain intensified, the tone was far different. I was quiet, focused, and hurting too much to say more than a word or two between weak breaths that passed from my dry lips. "Ice chips . . . back hurting, hold my hand." Stephen was as helpful as he could be. But in trying to be brave and strong, he did not show me his tears or emotions. That was the beginning of a pattern to follow for some time. He held it all in, and his way to cope was to sleep. I remember saying to myself with irritation and disappointment, "How on earth could he sleep at a time like this?" I would look at him as I labored and wonder how we could be handling this so differently—also a thought process I would wrestle with in the months that followed.

The nursing staff was mediocre at best, and their communication with us, and the support provided us was lacking. My room seemed to cool by several degrees upon their entrance. They brought with them no mercy, no compassion. Their interactions with us were awkward and strained. They acted uncomfortable being in our room, and it was apparent they had no interest in dealing with our situation, much less supporting us through it. In turn, we felt very uncomfortable when they came around us. There was a stretch of several hours when the nurses didn't even come in to check on us, and we felt very alone and isolated. Still, it was better than how we felt when they were present in the room. There was only one other constant in our room with us, and that was a doula (birthing helper) I had asked to come and be of support. She filled in the gaps, giving bathroom and coffee breaks to Stephen, and contributed greatly by sharing her wisdom and experience in birthing know-how: breathing, meditation techniques, and massages. And she gave a constant covering of comforting prayer.

I was having serious breathing and heart concerns. It felt like my lungs were filling with fluid, and I sensed pressure around my heart, but the nursing staff was not attentive enough to notice the severity. I chose not to receive an epidural, opting to go without the medications they offered. That had seemingly irritated them too. No one bothered to find out why I had made that choice.

I was thinking that if she were still alive, I didn't want the meds to add to her challenges and prevent her from making it. I was also mentally bargaining with God. "Lord, if I must go through labor and feel all the pain, please just let me have her when it is all finished."

"PLEASE CRY"

On December 20, 2001, after twenty-three hours of labor and an hour before our baby's birth, I stopped breathing and fell off the toilet to the floor, lifeless. What happened was, I had gone into shock after my blood pressure dropped lower and lower. During my pregnancy, I'd had remarkably low blood pressure, but it never seemed to raise red flags on my exams. Now, though, I immediately received more attention from the nurses in the next twenty minutes than I had in the previous twenty-three hours. They couldn't get a pulse on me. Codes were called, the crash kit was pulled out, and the alarm was real. I was gone briefly but soon came back. There were no immediate answers as to what had happened to me, and no one bothered to investigate—a baby was coming very soon, and we were all now focused on the birth. Several excruciatingly painful pushes, and she entered the world. She was lying there on the bed, and it seemed like everyone froze. Oh, the silence . . . as I stared down at her lifeless body I was screaming silently for her, "Cry . . . please cry . . . oh God, she's not crying . . . please open your eyes, baby girl."

It was the purest form of agony—my heart was instantly wounded, as if a sword had entered and been pulled out, and now I was left bleeding and slowly dying. That very moment a poignant shift in my life occurred. I became a mother, but to a dead child whom I could not parent in life. I was alive, but felt dead. My dreams and visions for our family would not come to fruition. I had no sense of security for a future I could create or what was yet to come. For the first time ever, I had lost all hope and the will to live.

Right away there was evidence for her cause of death. She had two umbilical cord issues: entanglement of the cord around her wrist and a Velamentous cord insertion.[2] The autopsy showed she was a very healthy baby with no issues otherwise. Sadly, I later found when requesting her file, a medical professional had seen and diagnosed the Velamentous cord at her only ultrasound at twenty weeks, and entered that information in her chart, but chose to keep it hidden in my file and never shared that vital information. When diagnosed on an ultrasound, this typically places the mother and baby in a high-risk category, and she will receive a higher level of managed care by her obstetrician. When a baby is showing signs of stress or growth restriction documented on the ultrasound and heart rate monitoring (Non-Stress Test), the physician would then likely intervene with either an induction of labor or a caesarean section.

FOUR HOURS WITH OUR DAUGHTER

We didn't know what to do next or how to best walk through the brief time we had with our precious little Grace, and the staff didn't serve as very helpful guides. As a result, we carry many regrets. She seemed quite fragile, and we were so scared to "hurt" her. She had some places called skin tears where her delicate skin had peeled, she had some dark bruising from the delivery, and her head had become softer than what a living baby's head would feel

We gave her up too soon.

like. Only a few photos were taken and no video at all. We gave her up far too soon, under pressure from the hospital staff to quickly say our good-byes and move from the delivery room into the recovery room. The only memories we have with Grace are built on four short hours of time with our baby. We didn't bathe her, see her naked body, didn't feel her skin against our skin; we didn't sing to her, read to her, or pray over our darling little girl. Thankfully, my husband and I were united in our desire to hold and spend time with our baby. However, we didn't snuggle and cradle her enough, and that still hurts my heart today.

I became a mom when I became pregnant with Grace, but I had no baby in my arms to prove it. Leaving the hospital, I was overwhelmed with feelings of resentment, seeing others who were lined up at the doors leaving happily with their babies as we got in our car, just the two of us. We had to leave our baby there, cold and alone in the hospital morgue. I turned and looked in the back seat where she should have been as we drove away and began sobbing, and I don't think I stopped sobbing for months.

Cards, flowers, food, and gifts filled our home. The doorbell rang often, and through the course of one week, we ended up receiving six assorted large containers of lasagna along with other forms of noodles, sauce, and cheese combinations provided by concerned friends. We mustered a weak smile at the door as the same meal arrived each day. After we finished off one pan, I turned to cereal and toast for my meals. Food had lost its flavor, and I barely could stomach it anyway. It was three days before Christmas and eight days before my birthday. We were planning Grace's memorial service that was to take place on December 27, 2001.

It was all a focused blur. At one moment, I was very aware of what happened to us and openly grieved; the next, I was in a fogged state and zoned everything out. I was there, but not. Also, looking back I can remember some moments so vividly and others are fuzzy and hard to grasp. Hours were spent in the shower sobbing, or in bed in the fetal position clutching the pillow. But there were important things to do to plan her service and so somehow we managed to make those decisions, phone calls, and appointments. We put together a beautiful service and had a warm and wonderful show of love and support from family and friends. We had an open casket, but only our family could go near her (now I wish I had allowed everyone to see her). Our family commented repeatedly on how beautiful and perfect she was. They were rather surprised as I think they imagined she would look unpleasant. She actually looked her best in the casket, which I have since found not to be typical from those I have met who share that their babies looked best right after birth. The funeral home applied Grace's makeup perfectly, and therefore the redness, bruising, skin tears, and signature red lips of a stillborn were not visible anymore. Instead, she had the perfect color skin and soft pink lips that she would have had were she born alive and was just sleeping.

It felt good to do something that honored her and to invite others to meet her. Only two friends ever saw Grace in the hospital, and no family was ever able to see or hold her in the hospital. The service was an important step in our healing and a ritual we needed to go through.

AFTER

Once all the holidays were past and family was gone, and it was just Stephen and me alone, it was like starting over. Everything was uncertain in my mind. What would the future hold? Would we ever be parents to a living child we created together? What would I do with myself? I could try to go back to running my business of being an art director and marketing consultant, but my heart was not in it. I just didn't care anymore. In fact, many of the things that held significance before no longer had value or importance. Our perspective was completely altered.

Only months before, 9/11 had occurred, and that had a huge impact on us. It altered how we planned to raise our baby and defined how we wanted to truly focus more on our family and the things in life that were important to us. But now she was gone. Now we both were looking at life in a whole different light. As we observed things going on around us and in our world, we felt a great deal of uncertainty and fear. Life was more fragile than ever before. The protective bubble we thought we had around us had burst.

All I wanted was my baby back, and the ache for her was pervasive. I wrestled with depression, severe anxiety, and insomnia for many months. My faith was challenged to the core and seemed reduced to only a few embers. No longer did my church feel like a safe place or a place of comfort. Instead, it was a place filled with babies and people who constantly bombarded us with hurtful platitudes. More often than not the sentiments were well meaning, but the comments, suggestions, and judgments pushed us away and led us to go the journey for a time without the church. We relied upon each other, new friends found through loss, and the few in our lives who seemed to say more with less.

The loss of a baby is devastating no matter what age the baby was at the time of death. That said, however, a harsh reality became clear to me early in my grief journey. Because my baby died before having experienced life outside the womb, and she never had the opportunity to interact with my family and friends, they had not formed a relationship with her and never bonded with her. We thankfully had some memories with our baby, but for our family and friends, there were no memories with her that they could share with us in the coming years of our life. As her mother and father, we simply would not forget her, nor would we "get over her," as so many had suggested.

We relied upon each other, new friends found through loss, and the few in our lives who seemed to say more with less.

We longed for true empathy and understanding. We were quick studies in the grief journey and rather than succumbing continually to the barrage of misguided comments from our family and friends, we sought out a new community and developed a family made up of other parents who were grieving the loss of their babies. These friendships were essential to learning how to survive the daily grind of life in light of our present reality of not having children.

But even with newfound friends in our life, we still yearned for our family and friends to come around in their way of thinking. We wanted them to be more supportive and considerate in their interactions with us regarding our daughter. It would take a paradigm shift in their thinking, and I realized we could not fault these loved ones of ours for their prior responses. Were Grace to have lived even a few months or years, there would have been photos of memories with firsts: "First time she smiled at Grandma," "First time she crawled to Auntie," "First time she blew kisses to my friend." These experiences would have allowed our family and friends to grieve more congruently along with us as they remembered their experiences with her. Shared experiences would have helped them more intimately share in our pain. They didn't have that opportunity. Had they, though, I believe they would have felt a sorrow more akin to ours. A sorrow shared is a burden lifted— this is true comfort to know others are missing our baby too. Instead, it became evident that the "idea" of Grace was missed, but the person was not. Due to losing Grace in pregnancy, we had to learn to cope with a cruel and sad reality of this grief—she was much easier for the world to forget.

YOUR TURN

1. Have you written out your story and the story of your baby or child's life? Journaling, blogging, and documenting your story can be very healing and cathartic. If the thought of mentally reliving the scenes and purging out your emotion onto paper or screen sounds too overwhelming, just try a few thoughts a day to express memories, emotions, and observations. You are in control of how much you write and when you need to stop.

2. Create a baby journal for your home that your family and guests can write in. Find a journal with a plain cover and buy a few art supplies to decorate the cover in meaningful ways. Or simply purchase a unique lined journal or blank page art book that has significance to you in the way it looks and feels with its design and texture. Invite your family and any of your guests to make ongoing contributions to your baby's special book. Anyone can write comments, poems, draw pictures, paste in images, and share thoughts of your baby and your family. For example, an entry by a family member could read something like this: *"We are all missing you terribly today . . . it was your due date, and we are sad without you here. This evening a butterfly landed on my hand as your mommy and I sat in the comfy big swing. We had planned to cradle you and rock you to sleep on this special swing your daddy built for your arrival so we could show you the sunsets each night on your front porch while you fell asleep swinging. As I watched the bright orange and pink sunset fill the sky, I felt like you gave us a kiss from heaven and my tears gave way to a smile. With love and hugs always, Auntie."*

3. Sharing your feelings and verbally expressing your emotions aloud allow your brain to hear your thoughts amplified and with clarity. One of reasons people go to counseling or attend a support group is that they can share with someone the thoughts, feelings, and emotions stuck in their mind. It is freeing to let it out. One way to release these pent-up emotions, and also hear yourself and evaluate your thoughts, is to record yourself on your phone with a voice memo or a video. Find a secluded place (the car is a good option) and talk aloud as if you are sharing with your counselor or support group members. Begin by saying what is hardest or most troubling for you right now. Share all the thoughts swirling around in your mind. Then listen or watch yourself. If you were a counselor or a member of the support group, how would you respond to what you are sharing? It can be surprising to hear. You may discover you speak very negatively about yourself or your circumstances. Do you hear hopelessness, anger, resentment, or fear? You can observe yourself in a new light with this tool. Try recording the same thing over again but alter the way you speak about your thoughts to be more constructive.

4

Loving Your Mate Well in the Midst of Grief

*When you incorporate the five love languages into
your relationships, you will find new perspectives on
how to connect and stay close to your spouse
and family as you grieve.*

IF YOU HAVE EXPERIENCED the death of a child, you know that
the grief experience puts tremendous stress on the marriage relationship. Both of you are grieving, but as we will see more fully in
chapter 7, husbands and wives often grieve differently. You might
find it difficult to understand why your spouse is responding the
way they are. The response can bring additional emotional pain
to you. This difference may create emotional distance between the
two of you. At a time when you desperately need the support of
each other, you may find yourselves drifting apart.

If the two of you were not emotionally connected before or
during the pregnancy, the death of a child could feel like the
straw that broke the camel's back. On the other hand, many
couples report that the grieving process drew them together and

> If you do not feel loved by your spouse, the sense of isolation may intensify your struggle with grief.

their relationship became stronger. This is obviously what we hope for you and your marriage. What you are about to read has the potential of making that a reality.

The deepest emotional need that we have as humans is the need to feel loved by the significant people in our lives. For those who are married, the person you would most like to love you is your spouse. In fact, if you feel loved by your spouse, the grief is much easier to process. However, if you do not feel loved by your spouse, the sense of isolation may intensify your struggle with grief.

A LOOK AT THE FIVE LOVE LANGUAGES

One of the difficulties in keeping emotional love alive during the grieving process is the reality that what makes one person feel loved does not make another person feel loved. A number of years ago I (Gary) published a book entitled *The 5 Love Languages: The Secret to Love That Lasts.* The book has sold over twelve million copies in English and has been translated and published into fifty languages around the world. Millions of couples report that their relationship was greatly enhanced when they learned the primary love language of their spouse. Let me briefly describe the five love languages and challenge you to make sure that you are speaking your spouse's primary love language.

1. *Words of Affirmation.* "You look nice in that outfit." "I really

appreciate what you did." "One of the things I like about you is . . ." This love language is simply using words to encourage your spouse. There is an ancient Hebrew proverb that says, "Death and life are in the power of the tongue."[1]

If this is the love language of your spouse, nothing communicates love more deeply than words of affirmation. Conversely, nothing hurts them more deeply than words of condemnation. For example, if you say, "You have got to stop crying. It's been six months now. You have got to get over this," those words will be like a dagger in the heart of your spouse. On the other hand, if you offer affirming words such as, "I think your crying is healthy. It's a way of expressing the deep pain that you feel. I know this is hard for you, but we are going to make it together," you have just spoken life to your spouse. Your words are like rain falling on a parched desert.

One wife whose love language is words of affirmation said, "The one thing I appreciated most about my husband was that during all those months of deep grief he never once condemned me, but always gave me encouraging words. I could not have made it without him."

2. *Acts of Service.* Perhaps you remember the old saying, "Actions speak louder than words." That's true if your spouse's love language is acts of service. It is *not* true if their love language is words of affirmation. By acts of service, I mean doing things for your spouse that you know they would like for you to do. It may include such things as washing dishes, vacuuming the floor, mowing the grass, running an errand, cleaning the toilet, making the bed, or taking their car in for an oil change. It may also involve bigger tasks such as cleaning out the garage or painting the bedroom. The important thing is that you are doing something that

they would like for you to do. However, I suggest that before you begin a major act of service, ask your spouse: "Would you like me to paint the bedroom, or clean out the garage, or . . . ?" If they respond, "No I'm not up to going through that right now. What I would really like you to do is . . ." now you have clear direction as to how you can effectively love them.

Mark said of his wife, Jane, "One of the things that made me feel loved after the loss of our baby was that Jane continued to fix our dinner. We ate out two nights a week, but Monday through Friday she always fixed a hot meal. I often wondered how she had the energy to cook when she was going through such deep grief, but it spoke loudly to me of her love."

3. *Receiving Gifts.* It is universal to give gifts as an expression of love. My academic background before I studied counseling was cultural anthropology. We have studied cultures all over the world, and we have never discovered a culture where gift giving is not an expression of love. The gift says, "They were thinking of me. Look what they got me."

The gift need not be expensive. Haven't we always said, "It's the thought that counts"? But I would remind you that it is not the thought left in your head that counts. It is the gift that came out of the thought in your head. A rose, or her favorite flower, will speak volumes to the wife whose love language is receiving gifts. But again, the key is giving gifts that *she* appreciates. If you are not by nature a gift giver, perhaps you should request of your spouse a list of gifts that would be meaningful to him or her. You simply say, "I'd like to surprise you from time to time, but I need a list of the kinds of things that would be a good surprise if I bought them for you."

One wife reported, "For one year after our baby died my husband bought me a red rose each month on the date when our baby was stillborn. Nothing could have spoken more deeply to me of his love for me and our baby. I will never forget those roses. At the end of the first year I told him that he no longer needed to bring me roses. I knew that he loved our baby, and that he loved me. So what did he do the next month? He bought me a dozen yellow roses and said, 'These are for you—the best mother and wife in the world.' I think I have the greatest husband in the world." Obviously, for this wife, receiving gifts was her primary love language.

4. *Quality Time.* This love language involves giving your spouse your undivided attention. I do not mean sitting on the couch watching television together. Someone else has your attention. I'm talking about sitting on the couch with the television off, the phones put away, talking and listening, and processing life with each other. If you sit on the couch with your spouse for twenty minutes giving them your undivided attention and talking about whatever they wish to discuss, you have given them twenty minutes of your life and they have done the same for you. Quality time is a powerful communicator of emotional love. For some people, this is their love language.

When you speak the love language of quality time, you communicate to your spouse, "You are the most important person in my life." On the other hand, when you are always busy doing something and never sit down to talk with your spouse, you communicate that other things are more important than her/him. When processing grief with a spouse whose love language is quality time, nothing can be more important than making time to have meaningful conversations with them. Some of these conversations will be about the baby, and how we have been feeling today and what thoughts have been running through our minds. Other conversations will be about different topics, but you are always open to talk about where you are in the grief process.

5. *Physical Touch.* In a marriage this love language is expressed by hugs, kisses, holding hands, the sexual part of the relationship, a hand on the shoulder as you pour a cup of coffee, putting your hand on their leg as you drive down the road. To the person whose love language is physical touch, those touches communicate, "I know you're there, and I love you very much." If, in the process of grief, you withdraw from them and fail to lovingly touch them, they will feel hurt and rejected.

Please do not equate sexual intercourse with physical touch. The language is much broader than that. In fact, in the early days of grieving, even when your spouse's love language is physical touch, they may resist sexual intimacy. The grief is too intense, the energy level is low, and they cannot bring themselves to be involved in sexual intercourse. Patience and speaking the language of physical touch in other ways is the most powerful thing you can do to communicate your love to them.

Bob said about his wife, Elaine, "One of the things I appreciated most about Elaine was that in the midst her own pain she would often walk up and hug me and tell me how much she loved me. Her arms around me were all that I needed to continue the process of recovering from our loss."

Out of those five love languages, each of us has a primary love language. One of the five speaks more deeply to us emotionally than the other four. We can receive love in all five languages, but if we could only have one, this would be the one that would communicate love to us. In marriage seldom do a husband and wife have the same love language. By nature we speak our own love language. Whatever makes me feel loved is what I tend to speak to my spouse. So if acts of service makes me feel loved, I will do acts of service for my spouse. But if that is not his or her love language, it will not communicate love to them as it would to me.

This is why we often get frustrated in our efforts to love each other. For example, a husband may spend his Saturday cleaning the garage for his wife, only to hear her say later that night or the next day, "I just feel like you don't love me. I feel so far away from you." In his mind, he has communicated love in a powerful way by doing an act of service. But her love language might be quality time, and the fact that he hasn't taken time to give her his undivided attention in the last three days communicates to her that he doesn't love her. Having good intentions is not enough. We must learn to speak the love language of our spouse if we want them to feel loved. Few things are more important than holding on to love in your marriage as you process grief.

HOW DO WE DISCOVER OUR SPOUSE'S LOVE LANGUAGE?

So how do you discover your spouse's love language? You will find the couples Love Language Profile at the end of this chapter. I would encourage each of you to take the profile, as it will help you to determine your spouse's love language. However, let me give you three informal ways of discovering your spouse's love language.

1. *Observation.* How does your spouse typically express love to you and other family members? If they are often buying gifts for others, that is an indication of their own love language. If they regularly spend lunch with a family member and talk, quality time is likely their love language. If they are always hugging

family members, physical touch is probably their love language. So observe their behavior.

2. *What do they complain about most often?* Look back over the years and ask yourself, "What does my spouse most often complain about?" The complaint reveals their love language. If you went on a business trip and came home and they said to you, "You didn't bring me anything?" they just communicated to you that receiving gifts is their love language. If your spouse says to you, "I don't think you would ever touch me if I didn't initiate it," they are telling you that physical touch is their love language. If they have said to you through the years, "We just don't spend enough time together. I feel like we're just ships passing in the night," they have just communicated that quality time is their love language. If your spouse has periodically said, "I can't ever please you," they have communicated that their love language is words of affirmation.

We often get defensive when our spouse complains, but in reality they are giving us valuable information. They are telling us what would make them feel loved.

3. *What have they requested of you most often throughout the years?* If, when you get ready to go on a business trip and they say to you, "Be sure to bring me back a surprise," they have just requested a gift from you. If your spouse says, "Could you give me a back rub?" they are asking you for physical touch. If they say, "Could you take a walk with me after dinner tonight?" they are requesting quality time.

If you answer those three questions, how do they typically express love to others, what do they complain about most often, and what do they request most often, you will likely discover your spouse's primary love language. Again, we encourage you to take the profile at the end of this chapter and use it as a means of discovering each other's love language. It can also be found at 5lovelanguages.com.

Once you discover your spouse's primary love language, the challenge is to give heavy doses of the primary and sprinkle in the other four for extra credit. Nothing creates a more positive emotional climate for processing grief than each of you feeling secure in the other's love.

YOUR TURN

- On a scale of zero to ten, how much love do you feel coming from your spouse at the present moment? Why do you think this is true?

- On a scale of zero to ten, how much love do you think your spouse feels coming from you at the present time? Why do you think this is true?

- By observing how your spouse relates to other people, what would you guess would be his/her primary love language?

- Based on the complaints you have heard from your spouse in the past, what would you guess to be his/her love language?

- Based on the requests that your spouse typically makes, what would you guess to be their love language?

- If you and your spouse both take the profiles at the end of this chapter, talk about your results!

- Looking back on the time before your pregnancy, how effectively do you think you were speaking each other's love language?

- Since the death of your child, while you have been walking the road of grief, how effectively have you communicated your love to your spouse? How effectively have they communicated their love to you?

We hope this chapter will promote healthy discussion between you and your spouse, and in doing so you will become more connected emotionally as you continue to walk the road of grief together.

LOVE LANGUAGES PERSONAL PROFILE
FOR COUPLES

Below you will see 30 paired statements. Please circle the letter next to the statement that best defines what is most meaningful to you in your relationship. Both statements may (or may not) sound like they fit your situation, but please choose the statement that captures the essence of what is most meaningful to you, the majority of the time. Allow 10 to 15 minutes to complete the profile. Take it when you are relaxed, and try not to rush through it. If you prefer to use the free interactive version of this profile online, please visit 5lovelanguages.com.

It's more meaningful to me when . . .

1	I receive a loving note/text/email for no special reason from my loved one.	A
	My partner and I hug.	E
2	I can spend alone time with my partner—just the two of us.	B
	My partner does something practical to help me out.	D
3	My partner gives me a little gift as a token of our love for each other.	C
	I get to spend uninterrupted leisure time with my partner.	B
4	My partner unexpectedly does something for me like filling my car with gas or doing the laundry.	D
	My partner and I touch.	E
5	My partner puts his/her arm around me when we're in public.	E
	My partner surprises me with a gift.	C
6	I'm around my partner, even if we're not really doing anything.	B
	I hold hands with my partner.	E

7 My partner gives me a gift.   C

I hear "I love you" from my partner.   A

8 I sit close to my partner.   E

I am complimented by my loved one for no apparent reason.   A

9 I get the chance to just "hang out" with my partner.   B

I unexpectedly get small gifts from my partner.   C

10 I hear my partner tell me, "I'm proud of you."   A

My partner helps me with a task.   D

11 I get to do things with my partner.   B

I hear supportive words from my partner.   A

12 My partner does things for me instead of just talking about doing nice things.   D

I feel connected to my partner through a hug.   E

13 I hear praise from my partner.   A

My partner gives me something that shows he/she was really thinking about me.   C

14 I'm able to just be around my partner.   B

I get a back rub or massage from my partner.   E

15 My partner reacts positively to something I've accomplished.   A

My partner does something for me that I know she doesn't particularly enjoy.   D

16 My partner and I kiss frequently.   E

I sense my partner is showing interest in the things I care about.   B

17 My partner works on special projects with me that I have to complete.   D

My partner gives me an exciting gift.   C

18
I'm complimented by my partner on my appearance.   A

My partner takes the time to listen to me and really understand my feelings.   B

19
My partner and I share nonsexual touch in public.   E

My partner offers to run errands for me.   D

20
My partner does a bit more than his/her normal share of the responsibilities we share (around the house, work-related, etc.).   D

I get a gift that I know my partner put thought into choosing.   C

21
My partner doesn't check his/her phone while we're talking.   B

My partner goes out of their way to do something that relieves pressure on me.   D

22
I can look forward to a holiday because of a gift I anticipate receiving.   C

I hear the words "I appreciate you" from my partner.   A

23
My partner brings me a little gift after he/she has been traveling without me.   C

My partner takes care of something I'm responsible to do but I feel too stressed to do at the time.   D

24
My partner doesn't interrupt me while I'm talking.   B

Gift giving is an important part of our relationship.   C

25
My partner helps me out when he/she knows I'm already tired.   D

I get to go somewhere while spending time with my partner.   B

26
My partner and I are physically intimate.   E

My partner gives me a little gift that he/she picked up in the course of her normal day.   C

27
My partner says something encouraging to me.   A

I get to spend time in a shared activity or hobby with my partner.   B

| 28 | My partner surprises me with a small token of her appreciation. | C |
| | My partner and I touch a lot during the normal course of the day. | E |

| 29 | My partner helps me out—especially if they know I'm already busy. | D |
| | I hear my partner specifically tell me, "I appreciate you." | A |

| 30 | My partner and I embrace after we've been apart for a while. | E |
| | I hear my partner say how much I mean to him/her. | A |

Now go back and count the number of times you circled each individual letter, and write that number in the appropriate blank below.

RESULTS

A: _____ WORDS OF AFFIRMATION

B: _____ QUALITY TIME

C: _____ RECEIVING GIFTS

D: _____ ACTS OF SERVICE

E: _____ PHYSICAL TOUCH

Which love language received the highest score? This is your primary love language. If point totals for two love languages are equal, you are "bilingual" and have two primary love languages. And, if you have a secondary love language, or one that is close in score to your primary love language, this means that both expressions of love are important to you. The highest possible score for any single love language is 12.

5

For Friends of the Grieving: How You Can Help—and Hurt

Supportive and loving friendships are among the most
valuable gifts for a bereaved person. A good friend who is
considerate and compassionate in their communications
becomes the trusted lifeline in the murky mire of grief.
They—you—have the potential to be such a powerful vehicle
for healing. At the same time, the closer the friend, the
greater the risk of causing the greatest pain and hurt.
It all depends on their words and actions.

YOU WANT TO DO the right thing for your friends in mourning. Yet in the grief journey, close friends *can* become strangers
while at the same time strangers met through grief's experience
can quickly become good friends. But can close friends become
closer? Yes, they can. How do you ensure your friendship will not
be lost in the shock waves following the death of your friend's
child? The answer is integrally related to your responses. Does
your friend perceive them as helpful or hurtful? Your words have
power, and your actions can speak volumes to the tender and broken heart of a grieving person.

First, a reassurance. If your friend is a grieving parent or grandparent, and you have noticed your friendship with them changing, turning stale, or drifting apart since the baby died, be encouraged that through your continual loving responses, the friendship can be restored and even grow stronger. Make a point to introspect and imagine your life being traded for theirs and allow compassion to flow from your heart as you ponder the pain they live with daily. It is impossible to fully feel all they feel, but you can imagine at some level how deeply it hurts and how you might wish to be treated were their circumstances to be your own.

IMAGINE IF YOU WILL...

"I could never imagine going through that!" Have you ever said this or heard someone else say this when thinking of someone's tragic circumstances? It simply hurts too much to go there in your mind. However, imagination can help at a time of crisis and sorrow. Imagination can foster empathy.

Let's do a little mental exercise together that can help you connect more to what your friend may be feeling and experiencing. Let's imagine something totally different than the loss of a child but still something drastic and painful. Imagine having a workout buddy that you meet with each week at the club and that you trained long and hard for a triathlon together. For a year you have supported and cheered each other on while lifting weights together. You swam in the pool, biked, and ran long distances together and really enjoyed each other's company. You are both so excited for your upcoming triathlon together. Then one day on the way to the club your friend gets in a tragic car accident during which they lose their arms.

It is awful to think of, I know. Stick with me, it's important. Just for a brief moment, contemplate how badly it would have hurt at the time of the incident to lose both arms. Now think about what kind of process your friend will have to go through in order to heal and return to their altered life. Each menial task will require so much of them. Armless is now their new normal. Attempt for even five minutes to do a few things without using both arms and see how hard it would be to do simple tasks, such as to tie your shoes, comb your hair, button your shirt or write a note. Then think of the disappointment they would feel realizing they would not be able to do the triathlon after all the training they completed.

Though you truly feel sad for your friend, you also feel sad for yourself. You still long to do the triathlon together and can't imagine doing it without them. You miss your workout buddy—the club is just not the same without them. You hope somehow, someday you can still find ways to be athletic together.

However, just the thought of the triathlon can upset your friend. They are frustrated, weary, discouraged, and can easily move into an emotional place of panic and fear. Think how it would feel to want your arms back but how futile that thought process would be. You can visualize prosthetics being helpful but you know they will feel different and it will take time to adjust to using them. Now, try to imagine phantom sensations that are common for amputees when they feel the limbs are still there. You can begin to imagine what it could be like to have no limbs and appreciate the complexities of rebuilding a new life with such a dramatic change.

The lost limbs, of course, represent the life of the child that was once a part of their life and now is gone forever. Newly grieving parents often say that they feel like their heart has been

> Grieving parents and grandparents actually experience physical pain caused by their grief.

ripped out, or they feel like the trauma of their loss is like having had their legs or arms chopped off. Grieving parents and grandparents actually experience physical pain caused by their grief. One minute their baby is there; the next minute they are gone. It often happens that fast. Their chest can feel tight and they can experience symptoms likened to a heart attack. Now after leaving the hospital without their child, they truly have to learn new ways to go about their day in order to survive. The absence of the child affects all aspects of their life. They will need to find tools and resources that help them, much like prosthetics would. You can help them with this, but no tool or resource will serve as a quick fix and each one takes time to work into their life to become helpful. A prosthetic can't be fitted and placed until the surface area where it is going to be attached is healed. Similarly, parents have to go through some amount of healing before they can feel ready to receive certain advice, and before being receptive to counseling, support groups, and implementing resources.

Parents in mourning get phantom pains too, when they feel like their baby or child is still with them. They can almost smell or feel them at moments. They even experience an ache in their arms that they can't explain. They feel disabled and have a sense of being overwhelmed and often are anxious about how to do life now. Now their household tasks, job, and interactions with friends require mustering all their mental, emotional, and physical strength.

The triathlon represents the commonality of interests that

made your friendship close. If you and your friend were pregnant at the same time, your friend may experience conflicted feelings about you still getting to have your baby. She may have a hard time cheering you on in your parenting journey as she sits on the sidelines with empty arms.

WHEN FRIENDSHIP IS BUILT AROUND YOUR CHILDREN

When you have a living child that is the same age or even close to the age of your friend's child that died, and your friendship was built around the life and activities of your children, then it may just take time for them to work through their sadness and jealousy before they can return to connecting with you again. Your baby is still here and theirs—is not. Think about that. They naturally may not be as involved in the same activities any longer or may take a respite from them for a time. Some activities can bring more pain, and some can be comforting.

In Suzie's case she was an involved mom in her local school's theatre program because her daughter starred in many of the plays. But after her daughter's death, Suzie avoided theatre altogether for over a year. That meant she also was not seeing or interacting with the other moms involved in the theatre program. In time, however, Suzie felt stronger and was drawn back to theatre. She got even more involved as a way to honor her daughter in support of a program that gave her daughter so much joy. On the other hand, Suzie's involvement in the school's royalty program (homecoming, etc.) ceased because it hurt too much to assist with that any longer. She had imagined her daughter growing up and becoming the queen of the court by her senior year. She did manage to stay friends with one of the other moms that she had met through the activity. That mom had gone through some painful losses in her own life, and, with understanding, she continually reached out with loving texts and emails. She worked hard to be a supportive friend. Her words of affirmation touched a special place in Suzie. She showed herself to be a trusted and true friend, and Suzie kept her heart open to that friendship.

Over time as healing happens and your grieving friend feels your support to help honor the life of their child, she will have the strength and ability to still love, accept, and celebrate yours. Two years later, Suzie attended the senior royalty program and watched as her friend's son was crowned king. Though tears streamed down her face as she experienced intense emotions, she felt peace and was truly happy for her friend and her friend's son.

WHEN NEW FRIENDS CROWD YOU OUT

Have new people seemingly infiltrated your bereaved friend's life and become close to them? Do you feel like you're on the outside looking in? If your friend has stopped responding to your messages lately, you may feel slighted. You might be asking yourself, "How can a stranger suddenly become such a good friend and seemingly trump a longtime relationship?" If you are feeling jealous and hurt, that's understandable. Your friend might not be as available to you right now and may not seem to need you or to be there for you like she did before the baby died. That doesn't mean there won't be a shift back to the way you related to each other before. It might just be a temporary season corresponding to her grief.

It might also be that the new person who has befriended them has satisfied a specific need for love. Their new friend is speaking their love language. In the past, your friendship has worked well without stress or trial and has been built on fun times and other common experiences—just not the grief experience. Remember, for a bereaved parent, their loss and the gravity of that loss overrides all else. They are radically changed by the death of the baby. So be sensitive to this and give them time and space. During this time, however, you can learn their love language and help your friend heal in the process. By learning to apply the specific love languages that your friend longs for (especially now in their grieving), you can grow to develop a deeper and richer relationship in the future with them.

SERIOUSLY??

I hear it over and over again in our support group—stories of friends and coworkers making hurtful comments to grieving parents. As Troy shared with the group, tears welled up in his eyes. The experience was more than upsetting. His wife, Becky, began to cry, and he tenderly ran his finger over her hand. He said, "People we work with came to our house last week and made the comment, 'So why do you guys still have baby stuff around? I thought you would have gotten rid of it all!' They knew this was our fifth consecutive loss and that we have only one living child who has special needs. They also knew full well that our baby had been born prematurely and only lived for a few short days. Our grief is so fresh." Troy shook his head in disbelief and his voice trailed off with "Man . . . " Becky finished for him. "We were so hurt. I felt like saying, 'SERIOUSLY?!' Then we had to make it through an awkward luncheon together. It was awful." The coworkers never apologized and did not realize that their prickly words were like stinging nettles on their friends' hearts.

Another member of the group, Joy, lost her baby at thirty-five weeks gestation. She said it had been a bad week. She had worked up the strength to ask how her sister's baby was doing, which was a huge step and a difficult question to ask since Joy's baby had died only days before her sister's baby was born healthy. Her sister said in a comedic voice, "Oh, he's fine, I guess! He's alive and kickin' at least!"

That wasn't all. Joy then told the story of a man at her workplace who said, after she had been back at work only a couple of days, "We are ready for the happy you to come to work. Get that smile on your face, get rid of the sad face, and get back to your fun self. We don't like tears or weakness around here."

The other parents in our group were aghast and in unison said, "NO way! That's awful! I would quit! I just couldn't handle that kind of treatment. I would contact your human resources department and file a complaint."

When I (Candy) was pregnant with Grace, my sisters-in-law were both pregnant and we were due within months of each other. Several other very close friends were pregnant too. It was really challenging to try to communicate with them after we lost Grace. I gravitated to a friend who had experienced a miscarriage, the year prior to our stillbirth. Also, there was a couple from our neighborhood who had delivered a daughter six months before us. She had a disfigured face, but after surgeries would be okay. These two friends were much easier to talk to after our loss than all our family and friends with new, healthy babies and children. In total, there were eight babies born to our family and friends shortly before or after Grace was stillborn. Before Grace was born, I imagined all our kids growing up together and all the delightful play dates we would have over the years to come.

How quickly that all changed when Grace was born silently. These parents had their babies, and their life was filled with the joys and trials of raising their children. I longed for what they had, and they were uncomfortable with how our story was a reminder that bad things do happen to good people. It was challenging to hold conversations when we got together. I was thankful that their babies were here safely, because all babies are precious to me and I wanted their children to be doing well. It was natural that their world was about their babies. Mine was too, but the fact that my baby had died made for unpleasant and awkward exchanges.

It's normal for parents to have difficult times raising their baby or child. There are sleepless nights, temper tantrums, defiance, lying, growing pains, and sickness with which you contend. I understood that they needed to vent and process their frustrations. Yet, as I listened, in the back of my mind I was thinking, "I would rather have Grace here and deal with that situation. At least you have your baby and you can work through this. My baby is gone forever. There are no second chances or re-dos."

> I longed for what they had, and they were uncomfortable with how our story was a reminder that bad things do happen to good people.

YOU'RE COMPLAINING ABOUT *THAT?*

I had no patience with trivial complaints: "Can you believe this hair color she gave me? I would rather die than live with this mess. You are so lucky! Your hair looks good no matter what! You have it made." (What I thought: *Lucky? I have it made? It's hair! Truly, who cares? I don't. You can change it. It grows back. You have options and you can wear a hat or a wig. I don't think you really want to die because of your hair color, but I feel like I am dying inside because I miss my baby so badly. You don't care about her, though. You never ask me or bring her up at all.* What I said: "Your hair looks good, stop worrying about it.")

Or:

"I am so sad that they discontinued my favorite show! I loved that show! So disappointing! I have to find a new show now. Seriously, that was all I looked forward to on Thursday nights! I know. I'm addicted. What's your guilty pleasure?" (My internal dialogue: *I really don't care about TV, I don't even have the attention span right now for watching a show. My brain is fried from insomnia and replaying how I might have saved my daughter and wondering if she felt pain, and I'm often thinking of what her life is like in heaven. I don't want to share my guilty pleasures with you. If I had any and shared them with you, I am guessing you would repeat what I say in the next conversation you have with another woman.* Externally I said, "Not sure . . . chocolate or coffee ice cream, I guess.")

Or:

"We just can't decide. A) Do a cruise with the kids or B) go on one of those all-inclusive vacations? The cruise has so many things for the kids to do and we can chill and not have to watch them. I love the idea of relaxing on the beach in one location. Seriously though, who relaxes on the beach with kids to look after?

Ugh, such a hard decision, right? I am stressed out trying to get it figured out and all booked in time for spring break. What would you do?" (My internal dialogue: *Is that sweat beading on my upper lip? My goodness, I am so uncomfortable with this conversation. Oh, to have the ability to be in your shoes and have choices. I didn't get a choice. My baby isn't here, and if I go on a vacation it will be my husband and me only . . . no baby Grace, no kids. What would I do? I would definitely NOT focus on how to get rid of kids. I'd be focused on what I could do with my daughter if she were here, and how to include her. That said, I've not been a parent to a living child yet, and maybe I am being too harsh in my thinking. Who knows, I might need a break from my child one day too. It's just difficult to conjure those thoughts in my mind at this time in my grief. I wish I could chat it up with you and turn off the sorrow and pain for even five minutes. I just can't be very present in this kind of conversation right now.* Externally the words came: "Hmm, I don't really know what I would do. I'm sure you will get it figured out and pick the best choice for your family.")

As I listened to people around me carry on about trivial and momentary upsets, I felt anger seeping into my heart. This was not my normal. Prior to my loss, I was much slower to become angry. I could brush things off and not be bothered as easily. I had very tolerant ears. Now, listening to those comments through the grid of my fresh grief, annoyed rebuttals and commentary would play out in my mind. I was thankful that a loudspeaker wasn't able to blast them aloud. *Seriously, this is your big worry and irritation in life? Do you not see me? Are you not affected in the least by our story? Have you forgotten already what happened to us and that our baby is not here? I would gladly take crazy hair, no TV shows, and forgo the vacation, just to have my baby in my arms. Do you not realize how many people in the world are going through terrible things? You have been blessed with so much, and yet you are so dissatisfied and miserable. You have your babies and your children. I wish you could hear yourself! Grow up!*

You can see how hurting people can hurt others and snap seemingly so abruptly. If you got verbally blasted and hurt by your grieving friend, you might have said, "What got into them? All I said was . . ." It likely wasn't just that conversation that upset them. It could be the accrual of conversations but something you said became the straw that broke the camel's back. If the private commentary in the brain of your friend is increasingly more agitated and they don't have a healthy place of release to deal with the mounting emotions, eventually things will bubble up and out. I was not sharing my internal dialogue with anyone. What my friends saw on the outside was a neutral poker face. Inside, I felt deep pain, and I dreaded the hurricane of emotions and irritations that welled up inside me when interacting with people.

Then I attended a grief support group, and as people shared their hurts, fears, and disappointments, it opened my eyes to the reality that my thought process was widespread among others who grieved their babies and children. It was liberating and set me free from the shame I had carried. I was relieved to learn it was normal to have these emotions and thoughts, and over time it would get easier to talk with friends and family.

WHEN YOUR FRIEND SEEMS OKAY BUT ACTUALLY THEY'RE NOT

You see your friend and she seems to be doing just fine. When you talk to her it sounds like she has it together again. You might be saying to yourself that she is strong and she is moving on now. You might feel encouraged that life is getting back to normal, and this grief thing is going to be all in the past. Don't be fooled. There can be good days and bad days for people who are mourning. Your friend can pull it together and put on a smile and try to be there for you for your birthday. She may have a great day at the office with you and hit her goals. She may spend a Saturday at your barbecue where she jokes, laughs, and seems like the life of the party again, but then what you don't see is when she gets in the car and falls apart, tears streaming down her face.

It was a month after my daughter died, and I had spent the day pretending I was doing better. I posted my feelings and observations of my behavior to my cyber friends in my online grief support group:

"I had lots of 'good' things to enjoy with friends today. Normally, it would have been the perfect kind of day for me and I would have had a blast. I went out to lunch and then later out to dinner and to a Broadway show with my husband and two friends. You would think with all that 'fun' I would have had a good day. I found that I was very moody and had feelings that were all over the place. I felt like I wanted to party, live it up, and forget everything. Then I felt an urgency to run off, get away, and hide. Alongside those emotions came anger, deep sadness, and quiet depression. I was exhausted by what normally was invigorating for me. The reason I was out with my girlfriends for lunch is because it was the same time I was supposed to be at my baby shower with them. And this evening it was the one-month countdown to my due date for having Grace. I kept remembering every stage of labor; the pain, fear, and anxiety of meeting my stillborn daughter was still so raw. I drove past a bunch of teenagers tonight all laughing and having a good time. I slowed the car to observe them and found myself longing for a place in time where life was much less complicated and I didn't feel the pain and weight I feel now. I longed for the innocence of my youth and the days of early marriage when it was just fun, laughter, and the whole world of opportunity ahead of us.

> "I longed for the days of early marriage when it was just fun, laughter, and the whole world ahead of us."

"I smiled and laughed an empty laugh while with my friends. I felt like a shell. I was so not there, but I don't think they could fully tell that was the case. But maybe they are smarter than I think and they just played along to try to keep things light."

If you could draw how a grief journey looks by using a stick figure riding a bike, the image would not show the person on the bike going from point A to B on the page in a straight line. It would first go downhill, then uphill a little, then down farther, then up more, then up more yet, then down, then up high, then in a few circles . . . you get the idea. By the end of the page, there would be fewer downs with more ups and straight lines, but still you would see dips in the road all the way to the end. That is the grief journey. That is what your grieving friend wants you to understand as they wobble along on their bike.

HELPING, NOT HURTING

So what is helpful to say and do? How can you avoid saying or doing the wrong things? What is offensive and what is not? What if you mess it up? We have some tools to help you navigate the valleys, hills, and curves of this grief journey. You can do this! You can be a friend who is counted on in the grief journey and who will be a blessing in your friend's life.

HELPFUL WORDS[1]

- I don't know what to say, but I'm so sad. We are thinking of you and praying.
- However you need us, we are here for you.
- We love you guys.
- We miss them too.
- This is not taken lightly; it truly affects us. Please know that we are all deeply saddened by your incredible loss.
- This world won't be the same without them here.
- We all missed out. It's not okay.
- The significance of your baby's life is so profound.
- This is the hardest news for a parent to have to face.
- I don't understand why this has happened, but I do know that this baby's life still has a purpose and their story will touch many lives.
- I can't fathom how badly you are hurting, but I want to love you well through the pain. I hope I can help somehow.
- Can I hug you? Can I hold your hand?
- What's going through your mind? What are you feeling?
- Can I look at your photo album?

- Can I go with you or have permission to go by myself to the grave to take flowers?
- Do you need space or do you need us to be close right now? If it changes, that's okay too.
- We want to honor their memory. What would be meaningful for us to do?
- We won't ever forget. He will live on in our hearts.
- She is treasured. She is always going to have a special place in our memory.
- I am thankful to know we will see him again in heaven, but right now that's a long way off and I can't stop crying when I think about him.
- You are a good mom and a good dad. You loved her well and would have done anything for her. We all know that.
- I know wishing doesn't do anything, but I can't help wishing I could hold her again.
- She was so precious. So beautiful.
- He was such a gift.
- I am thankful I got to meet him.
- I am sad I didn't get a chance to spend more time with him.
- Look at that butterfly. It makes me smile and think of her and brings peace to my heart.

HELPFUL ACTIONS

- To admit you don't know how it feels.
- To send cards or forms of acknowledgment on anniversaries and/or out of the blue. To offer delayed acknowledgment versus none at all.

- To say their baby or child's name and talk about him or her openly and often.
- To give opportunities for parents to talk about their baby and their feelings.
- To leave the door open for the parents to join you for events such as parties and showers but not pressure them when they decline. Support them in their decisions.
- To bring up your own infant/child loss if you have had one, and be open to discuss your pain with transparency.
- To offer and provide ongoing practical help for daily life in the months and years after a loss: bring meals, clean their house, watch their children, give parents a chance to be alone, mow the lawn, shovel snow, run errands, send them for a massage or to get pampered.

HURTFUL WORDS

- He/she is in a better place. *The parents feel their loving home was a very good place to raise their child—and their arms are aching for their baby now.*
- It's God's will. *Many bereaved parents hold the belief it was not God's will to have their baby die, and they feel it's a tragedy that happened in a world where bad things can happen to good people. They believe God did not cause it to happen. To say it is "God's will" can also imply this is God's judgment on the parents.*

- God has a plan and it was His perfect plan for this to happen. All things work together for good. *The parents may or may not believe in God, but saying this will definitely push them away from God. How can it be God's plan to hurt a baby? God is a God of life and not the author of death. He has plans to give a hope and a future. Right now, the situation is not good and it is hard to see that good things could ever come of this tragedy. Let them discover on their own the blessings and gifts that may come over time through their child's story.*
- At least you have other children. *The child they lost still had a special place in their life and is gone now. No other child can replace or fill that void.*
- At least it wasn't a "real" baby. *This is in reference to an ectopic or molar pregnancy or miscarriage. The baby was very much alive and real. This is insulting to parents.*
- At least you weren't that far along. *The moment they found out they were pregnant with that baby they began to love them, and they wish they had been able to get further along. This statement does not ease the pain.*
- At least you didn't get attached. *Oh, but they were attached.*
- If it's not perfect, you don't want it. *The parents felt their baby was perfect; and no matter what health issue the child had, they wanted him or her in their life.*
- It's not meant to be. *How can that be true? There is no comfort in this platitude.*

- Everything happens for a reason. *Right now it is hard to make sense of this and find a good reason.*
- You can have another one. *Maybe they can but maybe not, due to issues you are unaware of or they are unaware of. Anyway, that sounds like a long way off and it doesn't help now.*
- If your baby lived, then maybe they would have been "bad" or unhealthy so God took him or her. *This statement assumes the worst—about the baby and about God. There is no way to know about a child's future health. Even if the child were to have challenges, the parents would accept dealing with those over the death of their child.*
- What was wrong with "it"? *Do not call the baby an "it." Reference the baby by their name in your conversations. If no name was given, then say "your baby" or "the baby."*

HURTFUL ACTIONS

- Do not bring up the loss of your pet or someone else's death as to say it is a similar type of pain or experience.
- Do not ignore what happened by saying nothing at all.
- Do not pretend as though things are normal and just fine when they are not.
- Do not exclude or cut them out of group activities—or out of your life.
- Do not make decisions for them. Empower them with choices. For instance, do not empty out the nursery before they get home from the hospital because you think that will be what's most helpful for them.

- Do not express an attitude that parents should be over their loss by a set time. Bereaved parents don't get over their babies. They take steps forward in grief and find ways to carry on the memory of their child. Life after loss often requires finding a new normal. Strangers can become friends and friends can become strangers. The length of the grieving process is different for everyone.

YOUR TURN

- Have you ever said any of these words or done any of these things listed in the "Hurtful" list? As you read this chapter, did you find yourself reflecting on past conversations with your grieving friend that may have hurt them?

  If your answer is yes, you are not alone. Please give yourself some grace and forgive yourself. We all make mistakes! You can always go back to your friend and let them know you read this and it opened your eyes to how you have been communicating in a way that may have been hurtful. Ask their forgiveness and how you can make things better in your relationship. Let them know you are willing to learn how to do and say things that are more helpful for them. Ask for a do-over!

- Are you grieving? Have you been hurt? Or have you observed someone you care about who got hurt who is grieving? Initiate forgiveness by writing that out here. Then go to them and share your feelings or ask permission to discuss what it was you saw that concerned you.

I need to forgive you for . . .

I am letting that go because I don't believe you meant to hurt me. This is hard for both of us. I don't want that to create a barrier in our friendship. I care about us too much!

Reflect on this chapter and write your own examples.

HELPFUL WORDS AND ACTIONS

HURTFUL WORDS AND ACTIONS

6

Is One Type of Loss Harder than Another?

You couldn't quite put your finger on it—the feeling you just encountered. But it hurt. It's the feeling that some losses are "worse" than others—that perhaps you need to get over your grief because what happened to you wasn't really "that bad." Yes, you have a right to your grief and to your feelings. But you can't stop others from judging, from having opinions. Discover what's behind those views and how not to be the one who makes others feel judged.

WHAT DO YOU THINK? Is losing a baby at any gestation difficult, no matter how early or late in the pregnancy the baby died? Would you find it fair to say, "It is understandable that the parents will be sad and will need to grieve their early miscarried baby"? Would you say the same is true if their baby were stillborn? Or do you feel that grieving is much more difficult if the baby died after months or even years of life?

Let's take a look at five stories of bereaved parents. One by one they became vulnerable and risked opening themselves up to others they did not know in hopes of finding comfort and under-standing. They each came with different backgrounds, cultures, religious beliefs, and the influence of their life experiences.

1. Sue married Jim in her thirties, which was later than she had hoped because she envisioned having a lot of children and had wanted to start a family earlier in life. They were not able to get pregnant even with trying various fertil-ity treatments. At forty-four years of age she experienced an ectopic pregnancy, where the baby grows outside the uterus. They were never able to get pregnant again. They never did have children. Because of Jim's diabetes and other health issues, they didn't qualify when they sought to adopt a baby.

2. Mary and Mike were high school sweethearts. They suf-fered eleven miscarriages. They had no living children but still planned to try to have a baby of their own. They were in their late thirties.

3. Melissa and Kyle were in their forties and had experienced five miscarriages. They had five sons, but always had hoped for at least one girl and a larger family with a "quiver full" of as many children as they could be blessed to bring into the world.

4. Nila and Jason gave birth to four stillborn babies in the second and third trimester, between their twenties and late thirties. They ended up having two living children.

5. Jill was nineteen years old and had just gotten a divorce. Her baby boy had died of SIDS at six months old. When she woke up she found her baby was cold and unresponsive. They tried CPR and called 911, but he was gone. Their rela-

tionship crumbled quickly, and she was now grieving alone and with deep regret. She wasn't able to find out much information from the autopsy. She wondered if her baby had suffocated at her breast when she fell asleep. Jill blamed herself.

"THAT POOR, POOR COUPLE"

How do you think the members of the group responded to one another? Do you think they all had opinions for which of these situations were more difficult and which warranted a longer time of grieving? Was it hard for them to offer support to one another since they all had different situations? Did you find yourself considering certain stories harder or more painful to endure than others, or did you form opinions as to what couples should or shouldn't do? So many factors affect our beliefs and opinions. Unless they are challenged, most people's personally held beliefs will influence their answers to these questions and have an effect on their level of patience and support of someone in their grieving process.

Sue and Jim felt a total lack of validation in their grief. They had no support from coworkers and family members because their friends and loved ones would not even acknowledge that their ectopic pregnancy was a baby. Some people said, "At least it wasn't a 'real' baby." Sue said she felt like screaming, "Well it wasn't a 'fake' baby—it was a baby with a heartbeat, but it developed in the wrong place, in my fallopian tube, and it couldn't survive there, so I had to go through an emotionally painful D&C procedure to remove my living baby!" People in her life would ask her painful questions like why she didn't just adopt, why was she infertile and implied strongly she did something wrong in her life to have caused her infertility. Some went so far as to suggest they must not have been meant to have kids. "It's probably better this way—having kids is hard work and stressful. You are better off without them!"

Mary and Mike felt their family just wanted them to stop trying for a baby. It had been too hard for the family to watch them go through miscarriage after miscarriage. Mary and Mike said, "They think it is hard on them?? How about us?" Friends commented continually that they should figure out what was "wrong" with them, so they could get whatever it was "fixed" and then carry a baby to term. Mary and Mike had not felt comfortable sharing with these friends that they had already flown to five different states to meet with specialists and gone through a battery of tests, all with no answers. They found out they were both healthy and every baby was healthy—no anomalies or genetic issues were ever found. The doctors just told them to keep trying.

Melissa and Kyle had felt a total lack of support from all their family and many of their friends. Certain comments cut deep to their core: "You should be happy with the kids you have. You have plenty of kids." "You are getting too old to try for more—it's past your time to safely have a baby. You are putting yourself and your family in danger." Even worse, someone said, "If you want my opinion (they didn't), you have too many kids." Melissa said that her friendships were all strained because so many people in her life were critical of her decision to try for more children. They made their opinions known in whispers, cold shoulders, and the evil eye glares. She felt the stares burn through her heart, and eventually their comments made their way to her ears through the grapevine. "Why haven't they stopped trying when she had so many losses?" "She was foolish to let herself go through that. It's her own dumb fault." "It's God's judgment on her. There's likely some deep, dark sin in her life and that's why she loses so many babies."

Nila and Jason shared that they had been fortunate to be surrounded by a loving family and group of friends who were supportive through their four stillbirth losses. Personally, though, they felt out of place, as no one in their circle of family, friends, and coworkers had gone through so many recurring losses, especially not late-term losses. They felt an extreme sense of isolation even in the midst of many supportive people around them. They knew people felt sorry for them, but in some ways they hated that they were pitied and looked at as "That poor, poor couple." They longed for normalcy. Fear and hopelessness had taken a toll on their lives. In general, they no longer felt safe and didn't feel they could trust doctors or specialists anymore. Even though they had two children in their life, they knew they were overbearing, overprotective parents, and felt bad that their children had to bear the weight of all that came with being raised by two grieving parents.

> They felt an extreme sense of isolation, even in the midst of so many supportive people around them.

Jill felt shamed by people in her life who expressed their belief that she should never have gotten pregnant in the first place. They stated it was better for her that it worked out this way, since she and the daddy weren't good for each other. The message she received was that since she was young, she had time to have more. She was also dealing with extreme feelings of guilt. She cringed saying "SIDS" when people asked, because then came the prying and uncomfortable questions for which she had no answers. It made her relive the whole scene over and over again.

Which of these situations would you consider more difficult and warranting a longer time of grieving? Try ordering these from one to five (one being the most difficult and five being the least difficult). The intention here is to simply show you how easy it is to quickly go to that place in our minds and evaluate another person's story and place our judgments on them.

THE GRIEF-O-METER

We live in a culture that has a tendency to rate and place more value on one life than another, especially the life of a baby. At what point is life valuable? At what point is it a life? And did they contribute to this world and society? I'm not saying this is right, rather merely pointing out that these thoughts do exist. Thus the mental scale is calibrated, revealing what tolerance is then given for bereaved parents. From generation to generation people pass down these personally held beliefs and principles. Few people will challenge them within a family or in the culture of that people group. It takes someone willing to step out of their comfort zone and risk straining valued relationships and their status in that group for the better good. The rewards can be profoundly beautiful.

Though a person may have previously held the same beliefs, if they become a bereaved parent, their perspective changes. After tiring of the blanket statements about their baby's value, their poor choices to keep trying for more babies, and the platitudes of a family member or friend who sounds insensitive and uncaring, they will be forced to make a choice. Either they can speak their mind about how those comments make them feel, or take a less confrontational route and just distance themselves from those people altogether. But their previously held beliefs will undoubtedly be changed by their personal grief experience.

There is an incredible opportunity for new depth in relationships and greater connection if people are willing to get uncomfortable and stretch their minds to think of things differently.

> No one is to diminish the loss of another.

When facilitating support groups, I have to preface that our group is a safe place to grieve, to open up, and to be transparent. There are parents, grandparents, and supportive friends attending, and among the members of our group the stories span from very early miscarriages to the deaths of young children. No one is to diminish the loss of another. We as parents don't like that being done to us and we should not do that to others.

Without these rules and boundaries stated, even grieving parents will find themselves judging one another's stories and unwittingly placing value of where each one rates on the gravity of loss scale. Without addressing and challenging this underlying issue as a facilitator, members of the group can easily slip into these norms fashioned within them over the course of their life. The following is a statement made by one mom to another in our pregnancy/infant loss support group: "I ONLY had a miscarriage at ten weeks. I can't fathom how devastating YOUR loss must be" (speaking to the mother who just had shared that her baby had been stillborn near term). The mom who had the miscarriage was trying to affirm the stillbirth as a greater loss but at the expense of minimizing her own loss.

She also didn't realize the message she was sending to another woman in the group who had experienced three early miscarriages (six weeks to eight weeks along). That mom of three miscarried babies was internalizing that message and translating it to mean that her early miscarriages weren't very important compared to a stillborn baby. She apparently felt she didn't really have the right to be grieving them. Later she shared with me what went through her mind. "I was thinking to myself, maybe it's silly to be so upset and distraught? Maybe my losses were not as significant? They have gone though much worse, I guess. But I can't reconcile the fact that I loved my babies and I so badly wanted them. I guess from now on, I will keep them to myself and hide my grief from others." Do you see what a slippery slope this becomes?

I call this phenomenon the "Grief-O-Meter." There is a person who points their Grief-O-Meter at the bereaved and comes up with a number. "You had an early miscarriage and you are young, I give you a few weeks to grieve and get over it. But since you are forty and lost a young child to cancer, I give you a year to get over it and move on with your life."

The Grief-O-Meter works a bit like the speed gun that an officer points at a car to get a number. The speed calculation on the gun simply shows that the car is going seventy-five miles per hour, but it doesn't show who is driving the car or what they just came from; nor does it understand where they are going. When the officer pulls the person over for speeding, he or she bases the ticket on the speed. The driver must pay the fine or attempt to fight it in court. The interaction is usually swift. The officer hands you the ticket and you carefully drive away.

Grieving people can feel it in their spirit when someone's Grief-O-Meter is pointed at them. "They tell me I need to snap out of it.

Just try for another. Hasn't it been six months already? How long are you going to go on like this? We want the old you back! Maybe you should just go get some meds so you can just be happy again."

When you find yourself forming judgments, stop yourself! Take that thought captive and realize the harm you are doing if you allow that thought to take root. For then it will bear the bad fruit that comes forth in your words and actions. Instead, think to yourself, "I want my thoughts and actions towards my friend to be loving, kind, helpful, and supportive." Then choose wisely what you say and do.

THE LOVE BOMB

Have you ever heard people applaud in a support group? I have. Tara shared her story—a story of what love looks like to a grieving person.

Tara's second baby, born with anomalies incompatible with life outside the womb, had just died. Friends of Tara and her husband, Jeremiah, decided to make a surprise visit to comfort them. The friends scrounged up the money and took a flight from far away. Once they arrived at their home, they sat in the rental car for a moment, conflicted. "We thought to ourselves, 'What if they don't want to see us? What if they are too hurt to even want to talk with us right now? We didn't even tell them we were coming. Well, at least they will know we cared enough to come and give them a hug. That's okay, if that's all we do. We hope to at least just tell them at the door in person that we love you, we are hurting with you, we love your babies, and we just wanted to give you a hug. That will be okay with us if they need their space and don't want to spend time with us.'"

Tara said when they opened the door they were blown away. It was like getting a "love bomb." That very act meant the world to her and her husband. They had a healing time together with their friends. She took that experience to heart and now feels strongly that simply being present and available is so important. Now she and her husband try to do the same for others around them who are hurting.

YOUR TURN

- Have you felt anyone judge the way you are grieving? How has that affected your relationship with them?

- Do you feel there is a spoken or unspoken expectation for what you should be doing differently? What is that expectation?

- If you could speak freely with others about how you really feel about the judgments and expectations, what would you say?

- Being honest with yourself, can you think of times you have pointed a Grief-O-Meter at someone else? How might you view those people and others in the future?

7

Men, Women, and Grieving

We have come to understand and expect patterns in
grief responses specifically from men vs. women and in
relationships between a husband and wife. Though identified
as "normal" ways to grieve, they are not always beneficial
and healthy. This chapter provides insight as to why men may
grieve a certain way and how to shift the grieving process into
a new gear to attain deeper connection, intimacy,
and healing for the couple.

IN THE IMMEDIATE aftermath to the death of a baby or child,
both the man and woman cry openly together. They share raw
emotions with each other and the people around them. They hug
and cling to each other. They speak freely of their love for their
child, their fears and hurts. They can even feel closer to each other
during that time than ever before in their relationship.

Then, a shift occurs. It's not noticeable at first, but it happens with or without a conscious choice. One day the wife notices
her husband is no longer on the same page with her emotionally.
She feels he is moving on mysteriously from deep grief. He seems
okay, when she is not at all feeling okay. In fact, she wants to talk

about everything that happened and needs to process it more and he doesn't. This shift comes at different times for each man. When asked, men share in retrospect they can see when it shifted—in the hospital, after the funeral, after he went back to work, when his wife became pregnant again, when he realized there wasn't hope for any more children, when he chose a new hobby to fill the void. They remember the shift and they may even feel bad about it, but they do not have a solution for again drawing closer to their wife in their shared loss. They just suppose their way of grieving differently was somehow the way they were wired to survive and to keep their family afloat.

WHY THE MEN STOP PARTICIPATING

We've observed that couples will attend support groups or counseling together and then after a few meetings, the men stop attending. The variance that alters this pattern is when the man happens to make a connection with other men in the group (often due to similar jobs or hobbies). They will arrange to get together with them on occasion or meet as couples outside the group and will then frequent the group a bit more than they would otherwise. The women, however, continue for many months or years on their own. The ladies are more apt also to form close, lifelong friendships with the other grieving moms they meet in a support group. They will make arrangements for the couples to meet for retreats, birthdays, and even baby showers when their friends become pregnant and have more kids. If the wives had not pursued these relationships, the men rarely maintain the connection with the other men they met from the group.

So why do the men stop attending? This is their answer: "She needs this more than I do. I just came to support her at the first few meetings and though it's been helpful, I don't feel the need to come anymore." Though this is not received well at the outset, the women gradually accept this change. Eventually, most will release their husbands from their expectations to always grieve together and in the same ways they are grieving.

However, the men will often return when there's a special anniversary or holiday. Similar to their wives, they have a hard time with those special dates and acknowledge that it brings up the raw emotions again. This is refreshing and comforting for the women in the group to hear. They will even say, "That is the first you have

> The man puts his grief in a box on the shelf.

said anything about how you feel in a long time. I'm surprised—why don't you say this to me when we are alone?" The men shrug their shoulders and say, "I don't know why."

I believe it is because there is a sense of "permission" to grieve in the safe place of the support group. I also think it is because the man puts his grief in a box on the shelf. It is still there all the time, but he doesn't take it out and open it until he comes to a group or agrees to a designated time to discuss his thoughts and feelings with his wife. To open up about his grief is like shaking a bottle and pulling off the cap, and it bursts with foam spraying all over the place. If he leaves the bottle untouched on the shelf it ages nicely. It's too risky to open that bottle of emotions. With risk, however, there can also be enormous rewards. The rewards can include healing, closeness with their partner, and personal growth.

Grief-stricken that your baby or child will not or did not

survive, as a father, you may have sobbed and yelled out in hurt and anger toward God, toward the doctor, the person who caused them harm, or at yourself (this is so normal). When you desire to be a dad and expect to participate actively in rearing your child, it's normal to be despondent to the point of feeling utterly depressed when you can't change the outcome of their demise. You were created to be a protector and provider and now something totally out of your control has happened. You didn't get the chance to protect your baby or child from this. You would rather have given your own life so that your child could still be alive. Your plans to provide a secure financial future for your family can now lack purpose without the presence of the child for whom you were going to provide.

A state of melancholy, bursts of anger, and emotional shutdown are prevalent among bereaved dads. This deep emotional rollercoaster can last weeks to months. You may not daily verbalize emotions that your wife will express; or if you do, you won't express these feelings for the same length of time. Generally speaking, bereaved mothers express their feelings with far more words and tend to emote longer outwardly with tears than their spouses will. The emotions aren't necessarily different, though. More often than not, you are both feeling many similar emotions but they get expressed differently.

Of course, not all men fit the aforementioned pattern. There are always exceptions. Over the years of facilitating support groups, we have seen a moderate number of men who have cried at every meeting and were much more verbal about their emotions than their wives. Even years later they were still quick to cry at the mention of their child, while their wives were more phlegmatic and reserved. The men participated in the meetings even when their wives did not. These self-described "tenderhearted men" each ac-knowledged that they are the more emotional one in their marriage.

One mom, Kelly, shared that she couldn't even have her daughter's photos up at work because it was too hard for her to see them and keep a professional composure. She preferred to keep her daughter to herself and was more private about her grief. This is typically what we would hear from the men in our group. Kelly's husband, Don, on the other hand, proudly displayed his daugh-ter's photos all over his office and shared about her with anyone who would listen. Don loved to decorate pages in his scrapbook as a memorial to his daughter. The women in our group were inspired by his designs and would marvel how much he expressed his feelings openly and with such passion for his baby girl. They voiced in the group how they wished their husbands were more emotive and willing to talk about their feelings like Don did.

After reading this you may have conjured an image of Don . . . well, he is a police officer. He happens to have a tender, "teddy-bear" heart, and he adores all his kids, including his daughter in heaven!

When I've been assisting couples at the time their baby died in the hospital, I've comforted the fathers weeping and grieving deeply over their lifeless baby. These dads come to the support groups and detail how real their struggle is with deep depression after experiencing a miscarriage, stillbirth, neonatal loss, or SIDS death. When they open up about their feelings, the tears fill their eyes, and they don't make excuses for crying in front of others. I have held the worn and weary hands of men recounting the painful memories of finding their grown child lifeless after ending their own life. The love and hurt showed in their flushed faces, clenched jaw, and veins in their neck pulsing with the "why" and "if only" thoughts as tears made their way out of the dam. None of these men lost their manliness or seemed weak to those around them because of their tears. In fact, the opposite is true.

NAVIGATING GRIEF WITH THE LOVE LANGUAGES

Men and women can grieve both differently and similarly in the span of their grief journey. The times they grieve similarly do not coincide as often as the times they grieve differently.

It's beneficial in a marriage for the man and woman to have differences. Opposites attract and the marriage flourishes when husband and wife are not so alike. This is where iron can sharpen iron. It's equally beneficial if a couple has key similarities (a shared faith, common interests and aspirations), which serve as the foundational logs for the flame of their relationship. Physical attraction tends to spark the start of the relationship and serves as ongoing kindling. However, physical attraction is not the log of the fire that maintains the hottest embers through the wind, rain, and storms of life.

In personality, my husband and I are very different. I am an extrovert and he is an introvert. I am energized by interaction with people and he is energized by alone time. I am happy to sit and talk for a long while or go for a casual walk, and he is restless sitting for too long and has to stand and wants to run ten miles. He is a planner fiscally, and I am more carefree and trusting. But we share the same passionate convictions in our beliefs, and we love to spend time as a family and to be outdoors together. We complement each other and have a beautiful marriage. When our baby Grace died, we grieved so well together and we were so close, and then one day . . . we just weren't. We began to argue, blame, and hurt one another. We didn't grieve the same and we didn't understand each other's way of processing. It was through implementing the five love languages we were able to ignite the flame of our marriage again. Discovering each other's love language was an eye-opener. We utilized the tools it provides and began to build back the loving connection we had rubbed away, and it enabled us to appreciate and respect one another's different ways of processing what had been the biggest storm of our life.

WHY DO MEN GRIEVE LIKE THIS?

To understand the grieving process for men, we need to look back to the boy that each man once was. How was he parented? Was he able to grieve as a child? Boys are taught to be men early on. If he falls down, is sad over something, or gets his feelings hurt, he is often told, "Brush it off; you are tough. You don't need to cry about it. Suck it up and move on. Get back in the game!" This same message is given by many of the authority figures in a boy's life, including his relatives, teachers, sitters, coaches, etc. Right or wrong, this way of parenting is consistent across cultures throughout the world.

When that natural response to trauma and pain is denied and stopped, the child internalizes this and learns to buck up and bear with it and to force himself to quickly move on. This pattern of stuffing emotions continues for a lifetime if not addressed. The emotions resurface, more strongly, each time the boy, now man, sustains a new trauma, and it affects coping negatively. Stuffing works only so long—until the emotions explode or until the man silently slides into more unhealthy habits.

Why do some men appear to handle grief easier? Can a man truly not be affected by a pregnancy or child loss?

I have witnessed men grieve without emotion and with no tears. I have heard men say with a frank, matter-of-fact tone, "It isn't as big a deal for me as it is for my wife. She is really grieving and I feel more distant and not as connected to the whole situation." Why do some dads grieve deeply while others seem to "move on" and "get over it" faster? At the end of the chapter you will find a number of questions that will help provide greater insight into this.

HEED THE WARNING (DON'T GO THERE!)

When grieving, your emotions are raw, you feel vulnerable, and your love tank is likely on empty. You don't have much to give and your mate probably doesn't either. What happens when you only withdraw funds from the bank but never put any deposits in? Eventually there's a negative balance. The withdraw attempt will bounce. The same holds true in your relationship. If you can't meet her needs and deposit some love into her account the way she desires to feel loved, she may not give you anything in return. Just when you really need a loving hug and just want some connection with your wife, you receive a cold shoulder, rude comments, and a brisk verbal shutdown instead.

Far too commonly when there's hurt and rejection in a relationship, that's considered an excuse to tap into someone else's account. At the same time you are feeling slighted, you allow yourself to receive attention elsewhere. You suddenly grow close with a friend at work. In this friendship you find acceptance and a feeling of joy from this friend. She's nice. It's easy to talk to her, and she isn't sulking around like your wife who's crying or nagging you to do something for her all the time. There's no harm in hanging out with this coworker, you tell yourself. "I can handle this; besides, I just need someone to listen to me and make me smile." You start spending more time with her as she makes you feel good, and you spend less time at home. Before you know it—it's gone too far. Maybe not in the physical sense, maybe there's just an emotional connection at this point, but no matter what, it is too far.

When you are hurting and lonely, it is natural to be drawn to people and things you know are not good for you and could ultimately harm you or others. Yet how often do people give in, only to experience the awful consequences? Indulge in too many sweets and you feel sick to your stomach. Give in to a pattern of frivolous spending and quickly you are in debt and can't pay the bills. Yet we feel we can stop before eating too many sweets. We surmise that the transactions we make are fine. We know what we are doing and one more charge on the credit card won't put us over the top. We tell ourselves that we aren't going to fall into the same trap as others. We are wiser than that! We even say to people in our life, "I wouldn't ever succumb to the kinds of moral or fiscal failures I've watched happen to other people. The friendship at work is truly just a friendship, and it's actually helping me at home because it's making me feel better so I go home happier."

These enticements seem to offer an escape from the painful reality of your situation. But it will only make matters worse and cause turmoil. Don't go there! If she isn't your wife and she seems to understand you and comfort you better than your wife (who you just can't seem to understand lately and right now is just such a downer to be around), avoid your lady friend like she's the plague. Take the stairs if she's taking the elevator, bring in your coffee from home and stay at your desk if you know she is lingering at the coffee machine hoping to connect with you there. Invite your male coworker to join you in the meeting if you have to work into the lunch hour with her. More importantly, you need to share with your wife how your struggle is causing you to think, and share with her that you want help and accountability so you don't hurt her or your relationship.

> You are one positive conversation, one romantic date, one amazing night away from feeling deeply connected with her again.

Comfort and escape can call you from many different avenues, not just the inviting arms of someone else. It can be a bottle called spirits, or just one more can of hops to take the edge off. Hunting one weekend is one thing, but going off every single weekend will only drive a deeper wedge, adding to you and your wife's pain during such a difficult time. Even working out, which can be a healthy release for your stress, can still be taken too far. Anything that is done in overabundance or to escape isn't healthy.

Please remember this grief, these dismal feelings, will not last forever. You and your wife will experience joy and fun again together. Stay true to your wife and hang in there. I have seen the flame flicker and then ignite in more relationships than you can imagine—including my own marriage. It just takes time. You are one positive conversation, one nice, long romantic date, one amazing night of lovemaking away from feeling deeply connected with her again. It takes some learning, a shift in your thinking, and a bit of work but you can do it! It will be well worth your investment and you will find the dividends are huge!

The key is learning one another's love language and speaking it regularly. This will greatly impact the future of your relationship. You will find that grieving together can mean growing together. You have needs and she has needs, and, when grieving, it takes an extra effort on both parts to ensure needs do not go unmet because you both are hurting. If you each turn inward as you deal with your own pain, you send a wrong message of "I don't want you, I don't need you, I don't care about you, I want to be alone."

In turning toward one another, caring enough to help each other by loving the way the other needs to be loved, you shorten the duration of the grieving and you lessen the severity of the pain of loss because you find comfort in each other. You can heal faster as you feel the support and love you need to get through this.

YOUR TURN

Questions for Bereaved Dads to Consider

Your answers will shed light on why you may grieve a shorter or longer duration, and why your grief feels mild or more intense.

- *Were you parented with tough love? Did you have to stuff your emotions or brush off the pain when you got hurt?* If so, this is at the core of how you handle hurtful situations in life. Unlearning this and opening your mind and heart to be vulnerable about your feelings will be more demanding for you. Picture breaking new ground in the bedrock of your emotions.

- *Have you ever lost someone close to you before? A child? A parent or relative? A friend?* The more losses, the more arduous it can be to cope. It can also cause you to shut down emotionally and appear numb to the pain. Repeated losses in one's life beget loss of trust, which in turn begets fear and anxiety. Choosing to love is still the path to healing.

- *Did you get a chance to really process and grieve that loss? Or did you feel you had to push on and get over the loss of that loved one or friend quickly?* In light of whether you were able to grieve, or didn't have time, or didn't give yourself permission to grieve other losses before, then this most recent loss will feel formidable to address.

- *Did you want to have a baby and to become a dad? Were you excited about this baby?* The higher the level of anticipation and excitement, the more dismaying the letdown by not having that dream fulfilled.

- *Did you feel prepared to become a father? Or were you still coming to terms with the idea?* There can be a sense of relief that you don't have to deal with this, if the pregnancy felt too soon for you.

- *Were you worried about how a pregnancy would affect your wife or partner's body?* If relief is what you felt after the baby miscarried, simply because her body didn't have to go through the change of a full-term pregnancy, this is a superficial and temporary form of comfort.

- *Did you feel trapped by your wife or partner becoming pregnant?* If so, you might feel more relief than sadness over the loss—which can lead to conflicted emotions.

- *Did you get to feel the baby move when touching your wife's belly?* These touches allow you to grow in excitement and love for the baby, so if you didn't get the opportunity to feel the baby, you may feel more disconnected.

- *Did you get a chance to bond through participating in the baby's prenatal appointments or in their life at the hospital or in your home?* If you were able to see and hold your baby, the memories will be lifelong treasures. If your baby was too small or delicate to hold, or if they cried when you held them and you found it stressful or even frightening to hold them, you might actually feel more disappointed and angry that your time with them wasn't a positive experience. This can create a grief conflict in your heart.

- *Did you have a chance to really invest in your child's life and develop a connection?* None of what you gave was wasted. You now have the gift of those memories.

- *Before the loss, did you and your wife/partner have a strong, healthy relationship or was it strained and unhealthy?* If it was strong and healthy, be encouraged that you can build on that foundation as you grieve together. Like a tree that loses a beautiful branch, your trunk and roots are in place and you can still thrive. If your relationship was faltering and you were disconnecting before your baby/child died, it is possible you will be tempted to bow out and not work at tending to the relationship. That will only make matters worse. Allow the loss to draw you closer.

- *Do you feel some sense of responsibility for your baby or child's death?* Any guilt or shame added to your grief will impede your healing. It's critical you seek out the support, counseling, and prayer necessary to work through those emotions.

- *Were your parents involved in your life? What was your relationship like with them? Did you come from a good home or a neglectful and abusive home?* If you have fond memories of your childhood, you are likely to want a family of your own and desire to give your parents grandchildren. If your childhood was troubled, you may desire to "do better" for your children than what you experienced growing up. Or you may feel scared to be a father and repeat the mistakes your parents made. A significant loss can trigger emotions from your childhood that you weren't even fully aware of.

Grief Reactions: Check Yourself

These are normal reactions along with examples of healthy and unhealthy coping methods that are common for grieving parents. Write your initials and today's date next to each one that you are feeling now. Then in a month come back to this page and write the date and your initials next to the ones you are still feeling and place an "X" by ones that are getting better or are no longer an issue.

- Feeling out of breath, weighted and heavy, like an elephant is sitting on your chest. Sighing often. Frequent heartburn. You worry at times that you might be having a heart attack.

- Experiencing a sensation of arms being empty.

- Having an incessant need to check the baby room or the car seat.

- Unstoppable and continual flow of emotions that build up to unbearable levels inside the mind and heart that can eek out in outbursts: anger, fear, bitterness, envy, sadness, hopelessness, worry, anxiety, apathy, and shame.

- Crying all the time.

- Not being able to cry at all, feeling numb.

- Feeling empty and hungry all the time, eating constantly.

- Not hungry; food has no appeal.

- Sleeping a lot; always tired.

- Can't sleep at all.

- Hiding out in your home and never wanting to leave.

- Avoiding your home, staying away, never wanting to be home.

- Losing interest in your regular activities; everything feels grey and blah.

- Pulling away from friends and family; not answering calls, emails, or text messages.

- Struggling to stay on task at your job and with your hobbies.

- Escaping continually through fantasy: TV, reading, games, social media.

- Doing things in excess: spending money, shopping, gambling, working out, cleaning, taking on too much work or responsibility.

- Feeling the need for much more sexual intimacy and closeness with your spouse and need them close constantly.

- Not having any interest or drive for intimacy at all; don't want to be touched or to be near anyone.

- Absentminded, losing track of things.

8

These Shoes Don't Fit, but You Can't Take Them Off

The title of "bereaved" was not your choice. You didn't want to become a member of this club. But you are here now. This chapter provides guidance for the ongoing journey through grief, the rollercoaster of living out this "new normal." There's no finish line, nor is there an "Arrived" sign to hang on your door in grief, but there are healthy ways to embrace and walk it out well and with hope.

HAVE YOU EVER WORN a pair of shoes that hurt so badly? By the end of the day you had blisters and couldn't wait to take them off and toss them or donate them to the local thrift store. When your feet hurt, your whole body seems to hurt. When the shoes don't fit, it's nearly impossible to ignore the pain. Imagine a long day on your feet walking all over town wearing three-inch-high stilettos. Blisters begin to form and pangs of pain shoot up your legs. What if you tried "mind over matter" and declared to yourself, "My feet feel fine! They don't hurt at all." Would that make them feel better? Maybe that could work for a short while but not long term.

Now, visualize that you are stuck wearing those shoes every day for the next two years. Let's say you don't have any other options and you're just going to have to wear them and build up calluses until you increase your tolerance to the pain so you're able to go to work and go about your daily activities and errands. How would you feel about that? This is a normal occurrence for marathon runners and ballet dancers alike. Their feet can be covered in open sores underneath their shoes, but they cross the finish line and perform until the curtain closes. They can push through the pain for a time knowing that when they finish, they can address the sorry state of their feet.

Let's try on a different kind of shoe. These shoes are brown leather, lace-up, combat boots. Now, envision "boots on the ground," soldiers who are in the thick of a battle. In the face of danger they can't remove their boots. Even if they could take them off, there are no alternative shoe options on the battlefield. Even though their feet are hot, wet, itchy, and aching—they can't take them off. They have to forge ahead in order to stay alive and survive.

If you have experienced the death of a child, you are essentially wearing painful grief shoes that cannot be removed. This isn't a twenty-six-mile race or a four-hour *Nutcracker* performance. This is your life . . . and you are surviving a battle that doesn't have a designated ending point.

You didn't cause this battle and didn't even want to be fighting in it, but suddenly, you got drafted. You are on the front lines and now must figure out how to come out alive. Soldiers on the front lines can't just lie down and give up, because other soldiers are counting on them to do their part and pull their weight. You have other people in your life needing you to continue on and persevere. Though the soldiers on the front lines may all experience feelings of isolation and fear, they are consoled by knowing they are not alone and other soldiers are beside them feeling similar emotions. They find comfort in being "in this together." You are most definitely not alone. There are other soldiers who have suffered the impact of being at the epicenter of a battle characteristic of yours.

Who is your enemy in this battle? It's not the grief. It's not the shoes. In this battle the enemy is elusive, similar to guerrilla warfare where the battle lines are unclear and the soldier doesn't know where the enemy is coming from or even exactly who the enemy is. The attacks can come from any direction. When emotions incite a fight-or-flight response, you have encountered your enemy. When you feel hopeless, bitter, anxious, or fearful, you are engaged in the battle. Over time, you become more skilled as a soldier in this battle. You can recognize the enemy and eventually you will have the ability to recover and restore emotional territory. The enemy becomes weakened and no longer has the same strength and power to overtake you. The battle goes on around the world, being fought by other soldiers every day.

The time will come when you will finish this mission and take off your boots. You will survive with memories still strong in your mind. You will come through it and bear the title of "veteran." Civilians around you may or may not acknowledge how hard this has been for you. They may not fully understand the impact this has had on your life.

WELCOME TO THE CLUB

When your child dies, you basically become a member of a club you didn't ever intend to join; but now, you are a lifelong member just like the war veteran. The amenity, the perk of this club membership is the members themselves. They desire to help you—just as we have done with this book and with the organization I (Candy) started to help grieving families. Other members of this club have lived to tell the story, and they have good advice and insight to share in retrospect.

Just as a combat veteran may suffer from Post-Traumatic Stress Disorder (PTSD), a grieving parent may experience a similar struggle. After the trauma of the loss of a child, the experiences felt and seen are fresh in the mind for a long time. The battle still rages on in the mind. It's helpful to have outlets to share those thoughts and find out how others cope. The old-timers in this club have figured out ways to thrive, to be resilient, and to heal. They love to tell their story and they want to hear you tell your story. They tend to be very good at acknowledging and validating the significance of your baby or child's life. They can affirm that your emotions are quite normal. Though they cannot do the work of grieving for you, they create inroads and safe places for you and serve as lighthouses as you navigate grief.

On the other hand . . . whereas your bereavement club members who follow the club code of ethics will be considerate, careful, and not judging with their words, some of those outside the club will have sharp opinions for exactly how you should grieve. People might say, in essence, "Those shoes shouldn't hurt and you shouldn't be feeling any pain from them!" Seriously? But they are not wearing the exact shoes, with your same shape and size of feet, walking in your very footsteps on an identical journey! So they can't tell you how you should feel wearing your shoes! Their words imply that your pain threshold should be stronger! Sadly, this is one of the elements of the ongoing battle you will navigate as a bereaved veteran.

There are three harsh and alienating words that should never be said to the bereaved—but they get said, often. ***"Get over it."*** I hope no one ever says these words to you or places an unspoken expectation on you that you feel pressured to get over the death of your child or someone else's child whom you loved. If someone has said this to you or it was implied, it's understandable that you were hurt and offended. The nudge behind those words is for you to move past the state of grief you are in. It—is—not—that—simple—though, is it? The words presuppose that if you could just take off those shoes or that grief garment and put back on your "old-self clothes," or better yet, put on "new-joy clothes," then life would be better for you . . . and for them.

Certain "disappointments in life" may be processed with relative ease, especially when there is a replacement at hand (a lost job vs. better job, a missing diamond ring vs. a new ring). Even broken friendships can be replaced with better options and you might quickly get over the former when the latter is available (a backstabbing friend who gossips vs. a respectful and trustworthy friend; a physically abusive partner vs. a kind and loving partner; a careless and irresponsible employee vs. a careful and responsible employee). These examples help form others' (and maybe our) belief in the "get over it" ideology. Why? Because it worked for them in those other situations, so they assume it works for all grief, including the grief of losing a child.

The difference is, there is NO replacement for a child. The life of a child is remarkable. Your child (or grandchild) is your child for always. He or she had their own unique fingerprint and DNA. They will forever be very special and set apart. Their absence will be felt throughout your lifetime. Even if you give birth to another child, adopt another child, or already have other children, those children cannot replace or fill that space in your heart. It's actually very harmful to even place that kind of expectation on another person. It's impossible for anyone to fill the place of the child who died. No one can truly conform to the likeness of the child who died, nor can they fill the void in your life.

> You can be grieving well and in healthy ways and still have bad moments and still long for your child.

Grieving well is not commensurate with having "gotten over it." You can be grieving well and in healthy ways and still cry, still hurt, still have bad moments, and still long for your child. The meaning behind "getting over it" may be well intended or selfish; either way, you understand it's misguided and a poor choice of words. You need to communicate this fact in a way that will not push people away, yet will make them aware of how their words affect you. People who love you desire for you not to be stuck in grief. If you are depressed and hardly functioning, it is frightening to watch and concerning not to know how to step in and help you. Most often the person who says this wants you to be able to enjoy and partake in life again, which implies they think you presently are not. They want you to be happy again. However, only you know if you are stuck. Be honest with yourself. Have you been in a dark place in your grief for a long time? Are your thoughts now affecting your health, your faith, your relationships, and your livelihood? If so, let's help you make headway in grieving well. This will not require you to try to get over the child you lost, to love them any less, or to lose your passion for honoring their memory. This is about you surviving well so you CAN carry on their memory and *BE AT PEACE*.

You placed a high value on the life of your baby, on the life of your child that died. You felt he or she was valuable and worth dying for. *Are they worth living for?*

What about you? Do you value your own physical, mental, emotional, and spiritual health? Are you worth the time and effort it takes to be healthy? Is it worth it to you to take time to invest in yourself now, so you can accrue interest for your future self? Do you believe you have an infinite value and a life that has meaning? Do you see yourself as a treasure? I hope you will hear me if your inner voice is telling you the wrong answer. These truths are key to your grieving well and finding peace in your life after loss. You are worth it. You are a treasure. You have infinite value. Perhaps you're saying, "I don't feel very valuable. I feel helpless, hopeless, things will never be the same, and I'm not sure I'll ever be happy again." Those thoughts and feelings are normal responses when we have experienced the death of a child. However, healthy grieving involves acknowledging our emotions and controlling our thoughts. Grief is not simple and not one-dimensional. It involves the total person: emotional, physical, mental, and spiritual. While these four aspects of our humanity interface with each other— each affects the other—it is helpful to look at each of them separately.

PHYSICAL HEALTH

Obviously, physical health is fundamental to our well-being. While none of us are exempt from germs, infections, and accidents, we can take certain steps in keeping our bodies healthy. The three most fundamental issues are adequate sleep, healthy eating, and physical exercise. All of the research indicates that these three fundamentals are the most important things in maintaining a healthy body.

As you walk through the journey of grief, these three elements are extremely important. You may not feel like cooking, you may not feel like exercising, you may not be able to sleep well at night, but forcing yourself to be diligent in these three areas is one of the most important things you can do. Maintaining physical health, as far as it depends on you, is one of the keys to processing grief in a healthy manner.

EMOTIONAL HEALTH

Unhealthy emotions must be addressed as they arise or they will have the power to hinder progress and become serious roadblocks to entering into and maintaining peace. These emotions build upon each other. They intensify. They are like "weed seeds" in your mind and will crowd out healthy good thoughts. They will try to take over the garden of your mind, which then affects your thoughts and actions. Begin by learning to identify your feelings and negative thoughts. You might say, "I'm feeling hopeless." "I'm feeling angry." The thought that comes to my mind is, "I will never get over this." However, that is not helpful. "I will not be controlled by negative feelings and negative thoughts. I choose to keep walking. I will not give up." The moment you assertively take a bad thought and quickly pluck that "weed seed" from your mind, you replace it with a positive thought and then, a positive action. We are influenced by our emotions, but we need not be controlled by our emotions. Painful emotions will fade with time as we take positive actions based on positive thoughts.

We do not choose our emotions. They are simply the natural

responses to events that occur in our lives. Traumatic events stimulate deep emotions. In this book we have discussed some of the common emotions that arise when we experience the death of a child: anger, fear, worry, helplessness, hopelessness, despair, and depression. These emotions interface with our bodies. For example, disappointment and despair often trigger tears, increased heart rate, and high blood pressure. Extended feelings of depression often affect the chemical balance within the human brain. That is why extended periods of depression often require medication as well as counseling. Medication is designed to bring the brain back into normal balance, while the counseling is designed to impact the way we think about our situation.

The way to process the painful array of emotions after the loss of a child is to verbalize those emotions to family and friends who care. To suppress these emotions or try to convince yourself that you should not feel this way will simply prolong the grieving process. There is something about sharing painful emotions with others that allows you to breathe emotionally. That is why support groups, where you meet and share your journey with others, have been so helpful to thousands of grieving parents.

MENTAL HEALTH

While we do not choose our emotions, we do choose our thoughts and our actions. Our emotions and thoughts are interrelated—one affects the other. Emotions always push us toward thoughts and actions. Often they are pushing us in a negative direction. For example, if we have strong feelings of hopelessness and depression, those emotions may push us to disengage from the daily activities of life. The emotions may stimulate the mind to take medications to kill the pain. Many individuals have become hooked on opioids in an effort to avoid the pain of grief. Obviously, this is not a healthy way to process grief. I am not suggesting the avoidance of proper medication such as an antidepressant or antianxiety medication. If depression persists for an extended period of time, then conventional medication or alternative natural health supplements may be helpful. If one cannot sleep at night, then medicine may be used temporarily in order to get the sleep that the body needs.

Choosing positive thoughts leads to positive actions.

The various emotions of grief may push us to think that it is better for us to stay away from people because we are fearful we will break down and cry in front of others. The emotions of anger may push us to think that we need to lash out at someone whom we feel is responsible for the death of our child. The emotions of guilt may push us to think that *we* are responsible for the death of our child. We cannot keep such thoughts from coming to our mind, but we can consciously direct our thinking toward a more positive action. As humans, we choose our thoughts. I may feel like staying in bed all day, but I choose to get up, take a shower, dress fully, and take a walk around the neighborhood, have lunch with a friend, go to the support group, or attend a church service. Choosing positive thoughts leads to positive actions. Positive actions in turn influence the emotions. We feel less depressed because we got out of bed and did something constructive today. It is turning our thoughts in a positive direction, and then taking positive actions that lead to improved mental health.

SPIRITUAL HEALTH

Man is a spiritual creature. Unlike the animal world, man has an inner sense that there is something more to life than the physical. I (Gary) have an undergraduate and graduate degree in cultural anthropology. Anthropologists have observed cultures all over the world. There are no cultures that do not have a belief in a spiritual world. Something about man is different from the animals. Animals do not build altars and worship. Yet all human cultures are religious. There are varying views about God and life beyond death, but all people aspire for something more than physical existence. Both Candy and I have come to believe in the Judeo-Christian faith. We believe that the Bible, the bestselling book in history, is indeed a revelation from God about Himself and His desire to have a relationship with humankind, who was made in His image. It is our faith in God, as revealed in Jesus Christ, that has given us peace in the midst of life.

Here is what Candy says. "I believe it is possible to feel at peace even in the midst of trauma. I've observed this in others, and I have experienced it for myself. I have a peace that doesn't make sense in the natural world. It comes as a supernatural gift through my faith in God. I'm reminded of the words of David, King of Israel, 'Even though I walk

> "I find peace in trusting God with what I do not understand."

through the valley of the shadow of death, I will fear no evil, for you are with me.'[1] I know in my heart that God is with me. He comforts me and gives me peace. Though outwardly my circumstances do not have anything peaceful about them. Yet, internally

I can come into a place of mental, emotional, and physical peace. To maintain that peace I have to do my part. I have choices I must make moment by moment and thought by thought.

"One of those choices is to let go of what I cannot control. I can't control all the aspects of the battle going on around me. I can really only control my response and my own actions. I can't change the past, and I can't control the future. The 'Why' questions of the past do not bring closure or comfort. The 'What-if' questions do not bring peace. They leave one weary, exhausted, and anxious. I find peace in trusting God with what I do not understand. I have found His presence to be a constant comfort. It is what gave me the courage to continue life by walking into the future. I have allowed the pain of losing Grace to lead me into a lifestyle of helping others who walk through grief. I'll share that story in chapter 11. I am deeply grateful that God has walked with me through my grief process."

All of the common emotions associated with grief are addressed with hope in the Christian faith. Maintaining physical, emotional, spiritual, and mental health is the pathway to processing grief. Love yourself enough to grieve your way to health.

YOUR TURN

Draw a picture of what your grief shoes look like. Describe how your shoes feel right now.

What "weed seeds" do you need to pluck?

Fear. List each fear you are battling at this time. "I fear / I am afraid of . . . "

What would love say to you about these fears?
"Because I choose to love myself and others, I will . . . "

Anxiety. List your anxious thoughts you wrestle with. "I am anxious about . . . "

What would love say to you about these anxious thoughts?
"Because I choose to love myself and others, I will . . ."

Guilt. Do you feel guilty about something? "I feel guilty for . . . "

What would love say to you about this guilt?

"Because I choose to love myself and others, I will . . ."

Shame. Are you beating yourself up about something? "I feel awful about . . ."

What would love say to you about shame?
"Because I choose to love myself and others, I will. . ."

Start loving yourself well!
What is your primary love language? What is your secondary love language?
1). _____
2). _____

Knowing that is how you most like to be loved, what can you plan to do that is healthy and beneficial that will meet the need for love in your life?

9

Grieving Layers of Losses

Our history of loss and grief experiences is cumulative.
Grief layers will pile up, and it is necessary to address each
layer as it comes. One by one these memories and emotions
need to be identified and processed in healthy ways. Then the
flow of healing is possible. Traumatic situations will be more
challenging to process, but the earlier you do so the better.
The longer the layers stay buried, the more they become
hardened and painful to dig up. In this chapter, I share my own
stories of loss and how one affected the next loss. You may
identify. But it is possible to achieve sustained healing when
you are open to processing it all fully.

Here are two additional stories of grief from my own life.

I WAS VERY CLOSE TO my grandmother growing up. I was fortunate to have lived with her during part of my childhood; she
was more of a mom to me than a grandma. I remember fondly
the routines that I shared with her. Mornings included freshly
squeezed orange juice from her fragrant trees and loving prepara-
tion of homemade meals. My favorite was her German pancakes.

She made them by the dozen, and I managed to shovel in far too many to admit. Eventually, she taught me how to make them, a nostalgic indulgence for me that I have passed on to my children who now make them for me on special occasions. Perfectly thin and round and the size of a large plate, she filled them with fresh fruit picked from her garden and rolled them up just so. Or they might also be filled and topped off with yogurts, creams, jams, or syrups. (You can see why this is a special occasion meal.)

After the morning dishes were cleaned up and the animals were fed, we sat down to read the front page of the paper, followed by the obituaries. I would sit next to her either at the kitchen table or on the couch, watching what I thought was a curious practice. Was she looking to see if people she knew had died, or did she just want to see what age people were when they died? I noticed she would skim the announcements for the deceased who were eighty-plus years of age. If they made it to 100 or older, she exclaimed aloud, "Wow! One hundred and one! Imagine that!" I figured out that her head nodding yes as she read the obit was her concession to an acceptable age of death. When I inquired about this she said, "It's sad to see when a person has died, especially for their family, but at least they lived a long life." When she came across a younger person, she would exclaim aloud, "Oh my, she was only fifty? This young man, he was just thirty-five years old. This one, she was just a child, seven years old, poor dear. I wonder what happened." She would shake her head in disbelief as she contemplated the sadness of that loss, "My, my . . . what a shame," she would say—often uttering some words in German that I didn't understand. I wondered if in that moment, she was thinking about her own losses and family tragedies.

My grandma lost her son Dicky to cancer at age seven. She

had seven children, including Dicky, but she also lost five babies to miscarriage. She was widowed at a young age when her husband, my grandfather, died after surgery while still in the hospital.

Grandma was a tender soul, but a tough lady who survived many hardships and tragedies. At age sixteen she came alone by boat to Ellis Island to live with relatives in New York. Grandma said, "Moving to America saved my life and made you possible." Grandma explained that while she was still living with her parents in Germany, "They sent me away because they were concerned for my well-being but were never able to see me again." Her parents, my great-grandparents, had later prepared to join her in New York, but were killed in a bomb shelter in World War II. She was certain she would have been killed had she stayed with her parents.

"Please tell me more stories of your life in Germany, Grandma! Please!" Hesitantly, she would share, knowing these were difficult realities for a child to comprehend. She shared a memory of seeing people running behind her in terror from the fires from incendiary bombs that had been dropped. She had watched her whole world crumble under the destruction of the bombings and turmoil of war.

It would have been understandable if her wartime experiences had caused her to become hardened, cold, and harsh. Quite the opposite happened; she was the most loving, kind, and gentle person I've ever known. She had a strength and resolve that I admired, and an ability to press on and accept loss, all with a keen understanding that this world was not home—not our final destination. She poured out herself each day to help and to serve others.

Grandma died at age eighty-two—according to her, a long, good life, but to me, it was far too short. I wanted her with me much longer and hoped for her to one day meet my husband, to be part of my wedding, and to know my children. When I found out she'd had a stroke, I sat down right away to write her a long letter to tell her how much I loved her and what an impact she had made in my life. The snail-mail letter got there the day after she died and she never got to read it. That was beyond hard to hear. I was totally devastated. She was gone, and I didn't get to even say goodbye.

I was seventeen when my grandma died, and it was the first funeral I remember going to and the only dead person I had ever touched. I didn't want to let go of her hand. I sobbed so hard while holding her hand, it was soaking wet when I placed it back down in the casket. I wanted to feel the warmth of her touch but the only warmth I could feel was from my own hand. Her cold hands represented so many precious gifts of love in my life. As I held her hand, images flashed through my mind: all the hugs, the long back rubs and soft tickle that I loved, the braids in my hair, the hand-written cards for every special occasion, the beautiful vegetable and fruit gardens she weeded and fertilized, the knitted gifts, polka dances in the living room, the most delicious home-cooked food I'd ever tasted, the hands held in prayer while on her knees at the side of the bed, the way she cupped my face in her hands and looked deep into my eyes with a big smile, and my hand in hers as we walked to places in our community to take food and support to those in need. Her hands were so beautiful to me.

I tried to process my grief with writing songs and poetry. I

> I struggled to accept that she was really gone.

sang one of those songs at her graveside when she was buried. I struggled to accept she was really gone. I felt guilty for not being there for her when she died. At that time I lived a four-hour flight away from her, so I didn't get to be with her in her last days. I never got to serve her the way she had served me and cared for me. My whole family suffered in her absence. People were floundering without her as their rock, and the family drifted apart. After I returned home, I could barely function. I lacked motivation for school, work, and life. I was treading in churning waters of grief and losing strength to keep swimming.

DARK WATERS RISE

The waters of grief became more turbulent still with the call from my sobbing friend. I could hardly believe what she was saying to me. It was just a few months after my dear grandmother died, and my friend was telling me that her mom had just committed suicide. I was instantly propelled into rescue mode to help keep my friend afloat. I had to put my personal pain and struggle aside to help my friend. My girlfriend's mother had just told her that morning she didn't feel well. They came home as a family to a quiet house. Their dad called out for her, and when she didn't answer he went throughout the house searching and found her in the bathroom.

I went to the funeral and as I approached the casket I was trembling. Such different emotions flooded my mind. I couldn't bring myself to touch their mom's hand. I thought of my grandma's hand and it was so different. Here was fear, darkness, confusion. I looked at her face but felt like I was staring too hard.

With my grandmother, only good memories came to mind.

But this time "why" questions bubbled up from the waters. She was still young and had five kids who needed her and a husband who loved her. She chose to end her life. None of us understood her silent pain that must have relentlessly tormented her. We all were hurting, confused, troubled. But as with my grandma, there was no chance for goodbyes. No closure. We were left with regrets.

After the funeral, we reminisced and looked at photos, we retold the good stories and funny memories, and we cried until we laughed and laughed and laughed till we cried. I flew back home and prayed they would be able to heal and make it through their devastating loss.

Then something happened that shook us all to the core again just a few months later. The oldest brother lost his fiancée, who was pregnant. She was murdered by a past boyfriend. I sat frozen, in shock, in the second pew at that service. I replayed in my mind all that this family had already been through, and I couldn't wrap my mind around what had happened.

My grandma was my trusted go-to person in times of trouble. If she had been alive, she would have been the first person I called to share this news. I would have asked her to pray with me and for my friends. "What would my grandma do if she were me right now?" I asked myself. I looked up at the ceiling of the funeral home, vainly searching for her. My lips moved but the words had no audible sound: "Please help me . . . I'm scared. I don't know how to do this without you." I began to feel suffocated by the layers of trauma. I was aching for her more than ever.

I felt awful for what had happened to their family, but as much as I wanted to help, there was only so much I could do.

"WHY IS IT SO HARD TO LET GO OF HER?"

In light of these losses, my grandma's death felt somehow insignif-icant. I almost felt embarrassed to bring up my feelings about her. I reasoned to myself, "She was older and died after a stroke. There wasn't drama or trauma around her death. She is in heaven and at peace. I know she is okay and I will see her again."

Yet I couldn't help but ask, "Why is it so hard to let go of her and move on with my life?" I realized I never really fully grieved my grandma's death because I was suddenly catapulted into the other losses in my life. I was experiencing "delayed grief," which is an unresolved and postponed grief. It wasn't actually until years later that I took the time and energy necessary to grieve fully for her. When I did, I felt a genu-ine and lasting sense of peace and acceptance. For years I had no sadness, no regret, and no pangs in my heart at all when I thought about my grandma. However, when my daughter Grace died, I was instantly time-warped back to age seventeen, holding my grand-mother's hand at her funeral. I was longing for her touch and the comfort she was to me. I wondered if that signified I was opening an unhealed wound or that I was going backward in my grief.

It is normal for a new loss to trigger emotions from past losses.

I discovered that was not the case. Instead, I found that it is normal for a new loss to trigger emotions from past losses, even when they are many years apart. When grieving anew, we men-tally go back and touch upon our past grief experiences and then we assimilate the memories.

If you physically injure your body and then years later reinjure that same spot, you have a memory of what it felt like before when it was fine versus how badly it hurt after the injury. You anticipate what this will feel like now as you address it. You are familiar with the pain, and it's unpleasant to consider what it will take from you to get through this again. Even so, each physical injury is going to be unique to the body and to the person in that season of their life. Some injuries and surgeries are much easier to deal with than others. They heal faster or slower than before. You remember in the recovery process how you felt better over time. You have a memory of when you felt healed and free of pain. The same holds true with each new loss. We grieve with the awareness of how we grieved in the past, how hard or easy it was, how long or short it was to come through the grief, and what didn't feel good and what helped. We will gravitate again to the things that worked and helped us before.

When grieving my daughter's death, I had similar emotions reminiscent of what I felt before when grieving for my grandma and other friends and loved ones who had died. I said to myself, "I remember feeling this way before." I was keenly aware of how long it took to fully grieve and heal before, which proved both scary and comforting at the same time as I faced the aftermath of my daughter's death. I was scared for how long it could take to go through it all. I had lived through many other deaths of friends and acquaintances by the time I lost my daughter. The culmination of all the losses in my life created a grid from which I viewed grief. Yet there were also totally new emotions felt when my daughter died that I'd not experienced before, along with completely different life circumstances. Unlike when my grandmother had died, I was now a married adult with a supportive spouse at my side. This loss was not distant and far away. It happened to me, to my body and to my baby. I held my daughter's dead body, and I planned her funeral and I buried her. Losing my grandma represented a loss of comfort, protection, support, friendship, and counsel. Losing my daughter represented a loss of my future, the chance to be a parent, the loss of the miracle of a life we had created together, flesh of our own flesh, our baby. She was the gift I didn't get to keep. Grace's death superseded all other losses in my life and became the hardest thing I had to go through. Even though the past experiences of grief in essence conditioned me to be strong in the face of hardships and to develop healthy survival skills, nothing could fully prepare me for her death and learning to live life without her. Grieving my daughter was its own unique grief, set apart from the rest.

In the first days, months, and even first two years after Grace died, I was not able to picture being at peace and okay with her death. I still wanted her back. I still longed for her. I still dreamed about what life could be like with her. I was still upset that she died. I still had nightmares and difficulty sleeping. Anniversary dates hit me really hard. I had no other children, and I longed for a child. I battled fear and anxiety. This was concerning to those close to me, because it didn't look pretty. I cried a lot; I was angry; I talked openly about the hurt within.

But I came through all the healthier, having done the hard work of grieving. I could have done it in little spurts or put it on hold, but that would have delayed my grieving breakthrough. In time, I moved into a good place of peace. No longer did I feel anger or bitterness in my thoughts surrounding Grace. I forgave those who made mistakes that contributed to her death. I became thankful I got to have her for the time I had her. I stopped the futile wishing for her to be here. I could dream positive dreams again with hopeful expectation for the future. Though I didn't get to parent Grace in this world, she became the inspiration and motivation in my life for so many of my accomplishments. As I honor her through my acts of service, it is my way to actively be a mom to Grace on this side of heaven.

YOUR TURN

Did memories surface from various losses in your life as you read this chapter? Write down some of your memories that have come to mind.

List the names of each person you were close to who has died, or anyone whose death affected you. Note next to each name what is true for how you have grieved for that person:

Grief Was Delayed (GD), Traumatic Situation (TS), Didn't Grieve (DG), I'm Still Grieving (SG), Grieved Well (GW), I'm Okay and at Peace (OP).

It is important to see your history of loss and grieving. Be honest with yourself about where you may need to do some more healing. If you wrote "GD, TS, DG, or SG" after any of the names on your list, it will be of great benefit for you to set aside time to process each of those losses using not only the tools in this book but additional outside resources such as counseling and a grief support group as well.

10

Helping Other Family Members Grieve Well

You and your spouse are not the only ones who have suffered a loss. Grandparents, aunts and uncles, the child's siblings are all affected. Yet, as we have seen with friends, family may not always respond as you would hope. Here we offer insight for how to help your loved one who is grieving— and how to extend grace to those who are not being as helpful as you would wish.

"I FEEL LIKE I LOST two people—my grandbaby and my child," Valerie said in a support group. "Now my daughter is distant and pulling away, and I can't reach her. She and her husband are so depressed and withdrawn, and I feel completely helpless. I was so excited for this baby. I just don't know what to do."

Valerie is not alone. In addition to mourning the loss of a much-anticipated grandchild, niece, nephew, or sibling, family members sorrow for their own son or daughter, as Valerie expressed. Yet often their sadness is overlooked.

Of course, not all relatives are equally involved. But consider the grief of a grandparent who has been raising the child; an aunt who was the baby's daycare provider and was with them all the time; a twin sibling who shared the womb and their room; the grandparents expecting their first grandbaby; foster parents who were caring for the child.

If you were raised without supportive family members and no longer have contact with your family, or you have few if any family members still alive, then friends likely have become closer than your own relatives. Close friends can be ascribed family status—"Uncle Joe" and "Aunt Nancy." Bottom line, if you are "family," then you are family to the baby or child who died.

At the same time, family does struggle with emotions not experienced by friends. In previous chapters we have addressed the grief experienced by the child's parents, as well as the different patterns of grieving that men and women go through. We have also explored the helpful and hurtful words and actions from friends. Much of that material is still applicable and can be referenced for bereaved parents to use as they consider what will be helpful for their family. My goal here is to help loved ones—grandparents, siblings, cousins, aunts and uncles—better navigate their grief. Let's start with those who might, like Valerie, be experiencing the most pain.

HELP FOR GRANDPARENTS

Grandparents suffer a compounded and dual grief as they observe their child in distress, mourning for their baby. Simultaneously, they are heartbroken over the loss of their grandbaby. It is normal for them to put their grief on the back burner or to hide their grief while supporting their child. Watching their child go through this painful process is gut-wrenching for them. Here's more of what

Valerie was wondering: "Do I pursue and keep trying to help my daughter and son-in-law, or give them space? I feel stuck between a rock and a hard place. I ache for them and grieve the death of my grandbaby." Valerie's love language is acts of service, and she simply wanted to *do* something to help her daughter. Her daughter's love language is words of affirmation, so I suggested she begin sending loving cards, personal letters, and text messages to share her love for her daughter and her desire to do something to honor her grandbaby. This began to build a line of connection and helped her daughter open the door to let her mother into her life again.

> "Do I keep trying to help my daughter and son-in-law, or give them space?"

Grandparents greatly anticipate their grandbabies. Loving and involved grandparents imagine, long before their grandchild enters the world, how wonderful it will be to lavish their love upon them. They fully enjoy participating in the beautiful time of baby showers, decorating, shopping, and preparing their own house to be a safe and welcoming place for their grandchild. They look forward to babysitting and taking their grandbaby to fun places. They envision sharing the holidays and special occasions together. They expect to be ready to answer their phone at any given moment in case it was the call they had waited for . . . "She's in labor! Baby is on the way!" When the call comes they rush to the hospital, eager to be one of the first in line to hold their little wonder. They maybe even enjoy the honor of being in the birthing room to witness the new little one coming into the world.

Grandparents look forward to their chance to "do better this time around" with their grandchildren. I've heard numerous grandparents speak about how they didn't get to raise their child the way they would have liked, and thus have many regrets. Now, at a more mature and respectable place in their life, they feel better equipped to selflessly pour their all into loving their grandbaby. The child is the heritage and future of the family line. They carry on the family name. Their accomplishments make the family proud. Grandparents boast of what their own child produced—such a beautiful baby and later such an accomplished child! They are happy to fulfill the label of doting grandparent.

Grandparents may blame themselves for what happened, even though realistically they had no part in the death of the infant and truly have no power to change the situation. "If only I had been there, I could have done something to save them." They struggle with being alive when the child is not. "I would have taken their place. Why am I still here and they aren't? I've lived a full life and they hardly got a chance." These thoughts must be dismissed quickly and replaced with thoughts better suited to move forward in grieving. A more helpful way to process these feelings would be to acknowledge their sorrow and their longing to do something purposeful and meaningful to honor the life of their grandbaby.

The first grandchild is a new experience in the family. Firsts are intrinsically special and momentous—firstborn child, first words, first steps, first birthday, and so on. There is a hint of privilege that comes with the title of "first grandchild." The firstborn of each child in the family warrants a similar license. For grandparents, the additional grandbabies born after the firsts are not loved any less or considered less important. As more grandchildren come, there is a pride in the accomplishment of how their family is growing. But due to the firsts being set apart, the magnitude of grief can be intensified when it's a first grandchild. Fear of the unknown plagues their thoughts: What if this was the only baby they will have? What if they can't have or don't want to go on to have other children? Talk through these concerns and fears together with the parents. You can't control the future or the fact that these thoughts come to mind but you can control what you do with those thoughts.

Grandparents may feel a sense of comfort with the fact they have other grandchildren and they didn't lose their only grandchild. Even if your parents never voice this, you may sense this is what they think, and it can hurt profoundly. If your parents are not as affected as you believe they should be and don't seem to view your baby's death the way you feel a grandparent should, you may find it difficult to share openly or connect with them. Make the effort to gently express how you feel. Hopefully, over time, they can learn how to better support you and get more in touch with the gravity of your loss. If you see them focus all their attention on your nieces and nephews but they don't acknowledge your baby, this too can hurt. They may need you to explain how it will help you grieve well and still feel close to them, if they include your baby in things. Provide concrete examples of what they can do. Give them permission to grieve openly too. They may be concealing their feelings because they are worried it is too hard on you to see them so emotional about their grief.

HELP FOR SIBLINGS

On one of my visits to Grace's grave I saw a teenage boy sitting in a huge tree above the graves. It was a peculiar thing to see this boy up

"That's my twin brother's grave. Today's our birthday."

in the tree. I had not ever seen him there before. He looked away when I looked at him. I felt his observing eyes, though, as I placed flowers above the top of my daughter's marker and cleaned off the dirt that filled the engraving.

He broke the silence with a question. "Is that your daughter?" I replied quietly, "Yes, it is." "I'm sorry that your daughter died," he said gently. I thanked him. Then he began to share why he was in the tree. "That's my identical twin brother's grave, just a few over from your daughter's. Today's our birthday. I always come here on our birthday and spend it here with my brother. My brother died eight months after we were born, and I miss him. I feel the loss every day. This is my special day to come and just talk to him and hang out with him. Ever since I was old enough, my mom and dad let me have my wish to be here and spend some time alone with him on our birthday. It helps me a lot, and I like talking to him about everything. I know it seems weird. But it's not weird to me."

I was in awe. What an eye-opening moment for me to consider how differently people are affected when a baby or child dies. As a mother, I carried Grace and felt her move inside of me, she lived in me, and she was "bone of my bone and flesh of my flesh." My connection to her was closest, but I hadn't truly considered the ways others in Grace's life might have been deeply affected. How profound it was to consider the physical, emotional, and spiritual layers to how connected we are to our loved ones. I marveled at how this twin felt his loss on a cellular level. They shared their mother's womb and breasts and their lives were so closely intertwined.

Nearly four years after Grace was stillborn, I gave birth to our second child, and then three and a half years later we had our third daughter. Our girls grew up hearing about their big sister in heaven. They kissed her photo and hugged her bear and were swaddled in her baby blankets. Their personal drawings and paintings of our family always included Grace, who was stillborn, and later included baby Promise, whom we lost in a miscarriage. Every so often when a thought crossed their mind about their siblings, they shared it aloud. "I think if Grace were here, she would really enjoy playing this game with us. I wonder what Grace and Promise are doing in heaven right now. I wish Grace were here, so we could play together, I feel sad that I didn't get to grow up with them. Do you think she can see me at my performance today? She's lucky! She gets to fly. I wish I could fly. She never was naughty. She went to heaven before she did anything bad, so she didn't have to get disciplined. We would need a bigger car to fit Grace and Promise and we would have to share our bedrooms too, but I wouldn't mind at all. I'd like the chance to share with them."

We could have raised them never mentioning their siblings in heaven, but I had learned how detrimental that was for kids. I met many parents who shared that they regretted keeping it secret. When their children found out later in life they actually had other siblings, they felt cheated for having been lied to. They knew in their hearts there was another but had no proof—and it bothered them. Some children had dreamed about having a sibling and then found out to their shock that it wasn't just a dream. We wanted to be fully transparent and honest with our children, letting them express freely what they thought and felt about their own grief.

Everyone is shaped by both the good and the bad experiences of their life. A child who experiences the death of their sibling will be affected, but it does not have to negatively affect their life. I've observed children who have lost siblings are often more in touch with their emotions, compassionate, caring, thoughtful, and tenderhearted as a result of their bereavement. It's not a coincidence that scores of people I meet share how grief influenced their career choices. They wanted a career where they could help others by being a nurse, doctor, counselor, pastor, or social worker. Each described having lost a loved one or observed someone close to them who was grieving, and it started a chain effect that led them to pursue that kind of career. Grieving changes us and affects how we live our lives. We get to choose whether that impact will be for good.

Children experience similar emotions in their grief as adults. However, due to their age and maturity level at the time their sibling or loved one died, they do not yet have a framework for how to express and process their supersized emotions. If this is their first loss, then the shock and emotion of grief will be foreign to them. Experiencing a prior loss can prove either helpful (knowing they got through it before and survived it) or detrimental (they have gone through so much).

Younger children can accept the loss of their sibling and move on rather quickly compared to older kids and adults. When talking to young children about their sibling's death, use simple terms and explain the situation as best you can for their age. I heard a mother handle this very well with her five-year-old son when he came into the hospital room to meet his baby brother. He asked, "What's wrong; what happened?"

"Your brother's body didn't have a heart that worked the way it was supposed to. So when his heart stopped working, he died. Though I'm holding him now and we can see him, we will have to say goodbye to him soon because he's not alive anymore. Just like with Grandpa Joe, when we buried him and we blow kisses to him in heaven, your baby brother is going to go be buried and his spirit inside his body is going to heaven and we will blow kisses up to him. He will be with Grandpa Joe. We are all sad that he died and that's why we are crying. It's okay to cry and feel sad." The little boy kissed his brother and hugged him. He cried and expressed how upset he was that he didn't get to keep him and bring him home. He cried periodically over the weeks and months after, sharing with his parents that he missed him a lot, and he would cuddle his brother's bear and blanket. They would all cry together and hug and comfort one another. In a relatively short period of time, though, he was very accepting that his brother was in heaven. He had come to peace with his brother's death.

> The ability to receive emotional love endures far longer than the ability to express it.

The coping mechanisms of a child may frustrate, confuse, or worry you as a parent. Children will test you and push back on boundaries to find out if you really care and if you are strong enough to handle their behaviors. Their world feels scary and out of control, and they are reacting to that. Their behavior may rattle and shock you. These behaviors tend to rise up at inopportune times when you are already struggling to keep it together yourself. If your child is normally compliant to do their chores, diligent with their homework, and communicative about their day, all of that may change after the death of a sibling. They may be defiant, sullen, and reclusive. Rather than become agitated and engage in a battle, try to adjust your expectations and reactions. Approach them and the situation differently than how you would have dealt with those things before their sibling died. Treat them how you want to be treated. When you feel unmotivated, weak, tired, scared, lonely, or fearful, what are helpful words, actions, and responses from other adults in your life? Imagine what your child is feeling and thinking before you give consequences and directives. Give humor a try. "So you want to stay in your bedroom while we eat dinner—okay, well, we decided to join you. I brought a picnic blanket and we are all going to eat dinner in here with you tonight! I made your favorite . . ."

THE LOVE LANGUAGES AND GRIEVING CHILDREN

Families who grieve well together stay strong together in the long run. This is precisely the time to invest energy and time into your child with your genuine effort to love them with their love language (the Love Languages profile for children can be printed or taken online at https://www.5lovelanguages.com/). If their love language is quality time, carve out time to watch a movie with them, to play a game, to color, or to listen to the music they enjoy listening to in their hangout spot. If their love language is physical touch, then go out of your way to connect with them. Offer them a shoulder rub or back rub. Ask if you can braid or brush out their hair. Take time to hold their hand. If their love language is receiving gifts, start surprising them with little gifts each day. Make it a game to have them do a treasure hunt with a clue to find the gift for that day so they have something to look forward to each day. If their love language is words of affirmation, try putting up new daily sticky notes on their bathroom mirror or inside the cabinet doors in the kitchen that they will find with encouraging words, funny thoughts, and sweet messages of love.

Let your words and conversation be seasoned with

> Let your words to your kids be seasoned with gentleness, and remove any hint of pressure on them to perform to please you.

gentleness, and remove any hint of pressure on them to perform to please you. Show them unconditional love. Let them know you understand they need time to process this and to heal—just like you do. If their love language is acts of service, ask, "How can I help you get through this tough week at school? Can I help you study? Would it help if I picked you up, so you don't have to take the bus or walk home?" If they are not interested in talking, write a letter, text, or email them. Go out of your way to keep the lines of communication open and to stay connected.

Watching your child suffer through the turmoil of grief is like a battering ram to your heart. You may feel guilty for not being able to protect or keep them from the heartache of grief. The truth is you cannot control what happened. Beating yourself up with critical self-talk leads to negativity, isolation, self-harm, and self-hatred, and you will find your kids will eventually mirror your emotions. Firmly resolve to do what you can each day to be positive, and refuse to entertain thoughts that are detrimental to your healing progress. Focus on what you can control with your thoughts and actions that will help your children feel loved, safe, and secure. It is the small victories and breakthroughs for which you are striving. Moment by moment, then day by day, before you know it, you will notice it was a fairly good week. Things will get better. Hold on to hope.

HELPING THE AUNTS AND UNCLES

If you have siblings, it's safe to say they too have been hurting and grieving since the death of their niece or nephew. The severity of their grief will directly correlate to the kind of relationship you have with them and they had with your baby. Are you close? Were they eager to be involved as an aunt or uncle? Do your lives intersect at many points? Are they one of your "safe people" that you have turned to in the past during challenging times, calling them for advice, comfort, and support? If you answered yes to these questions, you are blessed to have such a loving sibling who cares deeply for you and your baby. They will endure with you, and you will help each other through the grief journey.

Certain life circumstances that are out of your control can complicate your relationship in the wake of loss. For example, if you were pregnant close together, there's a loss of the dreams you shared for your children. If your kids were playmates, you can feel guilt and sadness and they may feel disappointment. If your sibling has children and you lost your only child, you may feel jealous and they may feel guilty. Or if you and your sister had a history of a competitive relationship, you may feel resentful and they may feel uneasy and awkward.

The death of your baby can bring out insecurities and fears in your siblings. It's okay to acknowledge and address their concerns.

For example, if your sister is pregnant and your baby was stillborn, she may pull away and shrink back in fear that her baby will meet the same fate. If your response is to lash out in anger or to be short and hurtful with your words, your sister may worry this loss has changed you forever and that she has lost you, as well as her niece or nephew. She needs reassurance; she needs you to express your love and concern for her and her baby. If you sense this kind of fear, address it: "I have a feeling you are worried about your baby's well-being now. I pray your baby is born safe and healthy, and I want only good things for you and your

> "I need you to be willing to acknowledge my baby and not forget him."

family. Just because my baby died, it doesn't mean your baby will die. Stillbirth is not contagious. It's a false notion that my situation is going to jinx your situation. You guys are going to be amazing parents, and I look forward to being an auntie. I can't deny that I am going to also be sad that our babies won't get to grow up together, but in time I will learn to cope better with these raw emotions. I just need you to still be willing to acknowledge my baby and not forget him. That will help me feel a lot closer and safer in our relationship. I'm afraid my baby is just going to be forgotten."

WHEN SIBLINGS AREN'T CLOSE

What about the siblings that you are not as close to? Did you have a falling-out years ago, or were they divisive troublemakers who caused a lot of drama in your family? Maybe they are your step, half, in-law, or far apart in age from you and you never had a strong relationship. If they don't have kids and didn't ever gravitate to kids, they may not be as inclined to be an involved aunt or uncle. If they didn't make much of an effort to be a part of your baby's life, you can expect that they will not mourn the same as others who are close to you. You may feel sad about that, but you need to accept the fact that you can't change or control their response. They will not be missing or grieving in the way a close, loving family member will be.

In our hurt, anger, and bitterness, we can easily justify our negative actions. You have a choice. You can allow your difficult history with this person, and the pain you're already feeling, to pull you farther apart. Or you can use this loss to move toward healing the relationship. This could be an ideal window of time to reconcile. You know truly what is best. You will have a peace about what to do. If you have a distant or estranged sibling who tries to connect with you to offer support or condolences and their actions are heartfelt and well-intended, then find a way to put your past aside and open yourself up to grieve openly with them.

Now, if they have been abusive, toxic in their words and actions, and they are not safe or healthy for you to be around, then it's best to self-preserve and protect your heart. Begin by creating healthy boundaries around that relationship, especially during this vulnerable time of mourning.

SLOW TO SPEAK, EAGER TO LISTEN

Hurting people often hurt others, but that doesn't have to be the case. Everyone in the family is hurting. The death of a baby or child is considered one of the worst human traumas. Grief has the power to intensify other feelings and emotions. It's easy for people to say things in anger and to let things bubble up in frustration towards each other. But mindful restraint is a beautiful response and saves the people you love from the harm that hurting words and actions can cause. It is a sign of maturity and wisdom when a person is slow to speak and eager to listen. Too often we miss the intended message of the other hurting person. It is not only with words that we speak but also by what we don't say or what clues are given in our body language. If you don't want someone saying to you what you are about to say to them, take a deep breath, pause, and choose not to say those words. Ask yourself if there is a better way to communicate at this moment. Remember how meaningful it is when you receive a message communicated with loving-kindness. Make your goal in communication not to just be heard and understood but more importantly to connect with your family members in such a way that they feel loved by you.

For example, your mother says: "I sure hope you will be joining us for your sister's baby shower. She really would be hurt if you don't go. I think that's pretty selfish if you don't attend."

You might think in your head: "How could you even say that?! Why is it always all about her? What about me! I'm the one whose baby died. She will get to have her baby! I'm the one grieving. You are so coldhearted and the one who is selfish!"

Pray to find the best words and pause. Then respond with a message that's loving and helps you stay connected with your mom. For example, you could say: "That hurts, Mom. I don't know if I feel strong enough to go. I love her and care about the baby—it's just so painful for me even to think about a baby shower. I have the gifts ready. Would you take them in case I can't make it? I am trying to mentally prepare myself to go, but if I can't make it, Mom, please support me by giving me some grace for this situation. My grief is so raw and fresh. We were supposed to be celebrating our babies together. I'm just super vulnerable right now, and I don't want to be crying at her shower and detract from the joy of her celebration. I can understand how it makes you sad that I may not be there. I know we all wish that the circumstances were different."

EXPECTATIONS AND BOUNDARIES

The moment your baby or child died, your life was altered completely. Their death affects every aspect of your life—and yet much of your world continues on as normal. Your physical needs, home, job, bills, and family all demand the same attention and care. If you don't feel like eating, you lose energy, and eventually your health suffers for lack of nutrition. If you have surviving children, they still require loving care and to have their daily needs met. If there was a pile of clothes and dishes, it only grows in size and accumulates. If your house was in ill repair, it continues to deteriorate until addressed. If you are married, your spouse still eventually desires physical touch, intimacy, and connection. If your parents or other extended family are in your life, they too will have the expectations of you the same as before your child died. There may be some grace for you to be withdrawn and "to have your time of grieving," but ultimately, they will all still desire a similar relationship with you as before.

For example, if you are the one who has always checked in on your mom and dad and they look to you for assistance at their house or with doctor appointments, then they will still hope for that to continue. If you are the peacemaker in the family among your siblings, that will still be expected when they text or call you with their frustrations. If you are the one who plans all the special dates of birthday and anniversary celebrations, then you will feel that unspoken requirement to continue to fulfill that role.

You have a right to set new boundaries and to care for yourself and your own immediate family first. Initially, it may be an uncomfortable and difficult transition until you are able to establish a "new normal" standard with boundaries around your time and in the various roles you are willing to fulfill. This will require strength and courage to say and share truthfully what you can and can't do in this season of your life. It's helpful to let people know that "right now" or "for a while" this is what you need to do, but soon or down the road, you will hopefully be able to resume some of those activities and demands on your life. Ask them to please be patient and to have grace for you and commit that you will be doing the same for them.

You may find a need to create some new traditions around the holidays and special dates such as your baby's birthday and day of passing. Let's say Christmas is coming up, and you are feeling anxious about attending the big family gathering. You may have to tell your family that you can't do it this year and you are instead going away with your spouse to have alone time. They could be really hurt and upset. The most ideal response by your family would be, "Do what's best for you! We would rather have you with us and we will miss you, but you need the freedom to grieve the way you need to grieve." It's a real possibility that your boundary could set them off and they could lash out and verbally battle with you to guilt you into changing your mind. These are the sticky, messy realities of how a death affects the whole family and causes people to get triggered emotionally.

WHEN FAMILY STORIES EMERGE

Are you aware of your family's health history and any losses your relatives have experienced? There may be stories that come out now that your baby has died that you didn't know of before. People tend to cover up the painful past and sweep things under the rug or hide the evidence away in an attic or basement. You may notice some odd behaviors in reaction to your loss and it will prompt you to want to prod a bit into what could be behind that strange reaction. Grief tends to stir things up in a family, and the dormant and hidden stories get awakened and revealed.

I observed this to be true in hospital birthing rooms, which felt like an atmospheric pressure cooker. As families gathered together, still stunned from the shock waves of this death in the family, each was faced with their own history of trauma, loss, mental and physical health issues, and their surmounting emotions. All the painful memories that had been kept at bay, hidden and private, suddenly were oozing out like lava from a newly active volcano. This is one story that I observed.

I was providing photography and doula services for a mother who was delivering a stillborn boy. I sensed a thick tension in the birthing room, but I couldn't place from where the tension was coming. I just knew it was there. I felt led to ask, "Has anyone else here experienced a loss?" That broke the tension, and a high-pitched cry burst out from many family members in the room. Everyone was sensing the elephant in the room, but no one was willing to speak of it. The mother, who was resting between contractions as she labored to deliver her stillborn baby, explained why everyone was now crying. "My sister's birthday and death was forty-five years ago today. I didn't get to share life with my sister, and now I won't get to share in my own baby's life. My parents are a wreck because they are going through this again, but now with the stillbirth of their grandson. Their daughter, my sister, will share the same birthdate as my son, their grandson."

The grandmother was reliving her experience in her mind as she stood observing her daughter, and it triggered devastating memories. She didn't want the attention on herself so she had left the room, but her daughter really needed her at her side while giving birth. She was wishing her mom could put her own emotions aside to be present and help her through this birth. In the hallway, Grandma and Grandpa were sobbing and sharing their story with the chaplain, explaining how this had opened an old wound that never healed. They were instantly catapulted back to memories of not being allowed to see or hold their baby girl. Throughout the night she saw her daughter getting hundreds of pictures with her baby. She watched as she was able to cuddle, bathe, and clothe her baby, and the grandmother sank into a deep, dark place emotionally, embittered for not being allowed those healing moments with her daughter. Her unresolved grief from forty-five years earlier was unrelenting. Two months afterward, the younger mom stopped in my office to talk with me and shared that she felt she was doing far better than her mother. She was quite worried about her and asked if I could assist them in getting her mom professional help.

If your family member

> The more you invest now to heal your broken heart and come to a place of acceptance and peace, the better you will withstand the future storms of life.

doesn't seem to have a normal response to your situation, it may be that the death of your child has triggered a wounded part of them that has never healed from a past trauma or loss. They may have disassociated from the memory long ago and detached from their emotions. Take note, because you don't want this to be the case for you in the future. The more you invest now to heal your broken heart and come to a place of acceptance and peace, the better you will withstand the future storms of life. There isn't one thing that magically heals the soul wounds formed through loss. Inner healing requires your commitment to work at it and to be willing to release the unhealthy feelings that hinder your well-being (anger, resentment, lack of forgiveness, bitterness, hate, fear). Healing and peace can transpire over a much shorter time period when you have a strong faith, supportive family and friends, and grief resources, and when you are making healthy choices.

There are clinical terms and definitions that describe various aspects of grief. One term in particular that I believe merits mentioning is "complicated grief." This is different from what is considered "normal grief" and has far more intense symptoms. Grief is felt with a wide range of emotions from deep sadness, fear, anxiety, and dread, to shame, anger, and longing. Over time, it is expected that the intensity will ebb and the emotional state will improve. One sign that you are healing is that a sense of joy and purpose returns to your life. The grief "wound" will slowly heal and feel less painful.

On the other hand, complicated grief is an enduring grief over a longer span of time that is layered with intensified emotional pain. It is accompanied by irrational thoughts and dysfunctional behaviors. This grief wound looks raw, open, and never appears to heal and maybe even looks worse over time. When the pain is too great, some will become totally numb and disconnected. If you or your loved one is severely depressed, even contemplating ending life, then it's no longer normal grieving. It's now moved from normal grief to complicated grief. This requires getting professional help from a trained counselor or a health practitioner. Due to the cultural and societal stigmas associated with grief and depression, it's not uncommon for families to try to deal with their complicated grief internally. They regrettably often wait too long to get professional help. You may or may not be aware of the hidden grief stories and trauma in your family's history until you notice family members being triggered into what appears to be a complicated grief response. You might be saying to yourself, "I'm the one who lost my baby, yet my (parent, child, aunt, brother) is grieving worse than I am!" Each new loss adds weight to the unresolved grief from the past, and it's that much harder for your family member to cope with the loss of your baby.

YOUR TURN

As you read this chapter . . .

What unspoken expectations came to mind that you feel a pressure to fulfill?

What boundaries do you think you need to put in place?

Have you noticed any unusual reactions by your family members?

Do you think you or any of your relatives are experiencing complicated grief?

What are you doing or are they doing to get help? Is that working and proving beneficial?

What are the family traditions and activities you can visualize still being able to continue?

What family traditions and activities do you feel unable to do anymore?

What family traditions and activities do you think you will want to change?

Who in your family do you feel most loved and supported by?

What can you do to thank them and show them your appreciation?

Activity:

On a large piece of paper, draw a big heart with a cracked line down the middle to represent the heart that is grieving and broken. Above the heart write your name and your baby/child's name.

On the left side of the heart, write the names of your family members that came to mind as you read this chapter.
Next to their names write an emotion you think they struggle with (fear, anger, hopelessness, depression, need to control, overreacting).

On the right side, write their name again and write what you think is their primary love language, and also write what would be the opposite of the negative emotion that you wrote on the left side. For example, left side of heart. Bella—Negative emotion is fear. Right side of heart: Bella—words of affirmation, positive emotion of peace, feeling secure and safe.

Under the bottom of the heart, write your ideas for how you can help these family members by loving them creatively with their love language. Imagine ways you can help them begin to experience the positive emotion on the right side of the heart more than the negative emotion you wrote on the left side of the heart.

11

Unexpected Gifts—and a Legacy

This chapter shines light on the "beauty for ashes" in
my story, and hopefully it will help you ascertain the
redemptive beauty in your baby's story—and how you might
commemorate and honor his or her precious life.

IMAGES WERE FRESH in my mind of the frozen roses embedded in
the earth covering my daughter's casket. The chill from that frigid
day lingered in my bones. The longest month I had endured was
over. Breathing, but breathless, I reluctantly returned to work. I had
my own company with twenty-seven artists represented (graphic
designers, illustrators, photographers, and photo retouching specialists). I was their art representative. My job was to secure con-
tracts for their employment. Someone had to run the company—it
wasn't going to run itself. As the owner, quitting was not an option
at that point. The success of my business hinged on my leadership
and my operating with confidence and charisma, which I came to
realize had been siphoned out of me since my baby died. I pulled it
together just enough to function. My energy level was significantly
lower than my usual hummingbird speed. The energy expended to
accomplish little tasks was taxing. Initially, I'd do shorter workdays

> I felt like I had strange new glasses on with too strong a prescription.

and excursions and then, little by little, I could handle bits more. It looked like progress to most. By outward appearances, some people actually thought that I was doing well.

I stepped tentatively into the world to attempt involvement in a smattering of activities. I even managed to get together with a few friends. This took an incredible amount of exertion to pull off. Normally, this would supercharge me, but it was exhausting. I also felt like I had strange new glasses on with too strong a prescription. The world around me, my friends, and the conversations we had were so pronounced, so intense. Similar to when traveling in a foreign country viewing things for the first time and taking it all in, my senses became heightened. I felt like I was outside myself in an audience analyzing the scenes of my life. Moments were slowed and frozen as I psychologically took a photo of them. I observed and listened to people far more. *I began to see and hear the world through this grief lens. This was an unexpected **gift** from Grace—I was noticing important details I had missed before.*

At home, encapsulated in my grief cocoon, I could be found wearing my frumpy-comfy clothes, pets all snuggled in, and two quintessential food groups close at hand (chips and chocolate). I was drawn into a new world of online grief support groups, a world unfamiliar to me prior to having Grace. I found the other moms online to be refreshingly real and honest about their feelings. The scenarios they described having to muster through were tandem with my own experiences. No matter what time of day I posted, someone responded with empathy and love.

THE FIVE LOVE LANGUAGES: A FOUNDATIONAL TOOL

I was introduced to *The 5 Love Languages* as it came across my feed several times as a helpful resource. I read the book and took the test to figure out my love language. Then my husband also took the test. It was comical, actually, to reflect on how we had loved each other the ways we personally wanted to be loved. This worked well overall when everything was hunky-dory, with no major stressors in our newlywed life. However, it didn't work out so well for us once we both felt hurtful emotions escalating in the wake of our daughter's death. We were easily triggered and irritated with each other. My husband's primary love language is words of affirmation, and the runner-up is physical touch. My primary love language is acts of service, and quality time comes in close behind. Opposites attract, right? Well, the tools from the book were just what we needed to oil the squeaky parts in our marriage. We began loving each other in light of this newfound information and it helped tremendously. ***The five love languages became a foundational tool in our lives.*** This is a precious ***gift*** on our grief journey that helps keep our marriage strong.

Interestingly, prior to this, I had little value for the words of affirmation love language. It certainly was kind of you to say nice things. I preferred kind words to mean and hurtful words, but overall and deep down, I felt that words were rather cheap. If you meant something, then you backed it with your actions and you gave your time fulfilling what you said you would do. That's how I showed love. I had not ever valued when others tried to love me with words. You could say or write all the nicest things, but if your actions weren't congruent, then your words meant peanuts to me. I felt people's words too often were used to manipulate, to get something, to skirt an issue, to control, or to posture oneself in a light they wanted to be seen in. That mindset sadly came through personal experiences in life, and words eventually got a bad rap.

My perspective, however, changed dramatically with my involvement reading parents' stories online. They shared and were vulnerable for no gain other than to be heard and have someone journey alongside them as they grieved. I realized I wanted that too. As they opened up their hearts for their babies in their posts, I was inspired to do the same. I marveled how their words so eloquently painted meaningful images in poems, songs, and stories. I began to work the weak muscle of the words of affirmation love language as I would write and write and write. At the same time I became aware of the value in understanding each love language and the benefit of respect and appreciation for each love language.

When I saw a post from the online support group appear on my screen, my fingers picked up speed at the keyboard. I could not be with them in person to serve and spend time with them but I found ways to say with words what was in my heart to help them. I hadn't loved people with words that way before and it felt good to see the power of loving words in action. ***Words were elevated to a new level with meaning and life that I'd never known before.*** This is *a gift* from Grace.

A NEW WORLD OPENS UP

I found a new creative outlet through designing a personal memorial website for Grace. I titled the home page "Missing Grace." I shared her story, and my husband shared his perspective on a page he titled "Dad's Story." Resources I had found helpful were listed in detail. I added a few of the pictures of her and our family. I had a guestbook that people from all over the world started signing.

They left thoughtful, comforting, and thankful sentiments. They shared their stories and I treasured each one. I replied to every guest, and as I did my little world grew vastly. I now had online friends in places I'd never been or even heard of before. This all happened in the course of a few months after Grace was born. Shortly thereafter, Missing Grace gave way to birth The Missing GRACE Organization. I created a whole new website for the organization. Initially, it was simply an organization that provided online and phone support for parents who had a stillbirth. I didn't realize at the time how this would lead to a whole new career path in my life. Eventually, I would end up closing the doors to my company. My time, energy, and resources had shifted and were now funneling into our organization.

In the midst of so many good things, there was still a deep hurt surrounding the unanswered questions about my baby's autopsy, and fears in considering what might happen if I had another baby. The answers were not forthcoming from the physicians I contacted. So, I turned to my online bereavement community to see if they had suggestions, and amazingly, there were quite a few women who wrote nearly identical testimonies of how a particular doctor had helped them. They referred me to an OB/GYN doctor named Dr. Collins, who had dedicated his life to the study of what causes stillbirth and its prevention. They said how helpful and kind he was, with such a wealth of information. The next day he answered my call and we spoke for an hour. He gave me hope. He validated my concerns. He showed me a way I could help save other babies from stillbirth. It changed the trajectory of my life. I had a new mission. *I desired for Grace to have* **a lasting legacy** *and for her death not to be in vain.* I began to focus on how changes could be made to prevent others from having a stillbirth and in the process honor her story.

There may be policies or procedures in place (at your hospital, clinic, county, state, or workplace) that are not necessarily good, fair, or right for the bereaved. In fact, they may need to be addressed, challenged, and changed. *One of the most beautiful legacies the bereaved can create for their loved one is to initiate positive change in detrimental policies and procedures so others can benefit and be assisted better in the future. You don't have to be an expert to start! You simply need internal drive and tenacity with a touch of crazy, perhaps!*

I embarked on this uphill road using the vehicle of snail mail and email letters. I requested an opportunity for Dr. Collins to present a CME / CEU talk and grand rounds at the hospital. Another mom of a stillborn in my online group had a similar desire and she wrote to her hospital also. The hospitals both accepted. When Dr. Collins came to speak, we reached over 150 doctors, nurses, and EMTs with lifesaving education. Part of the presentation included sharing the story of our stillborn babies as well. The evaluation remarks on the forms made our hearts leap for joy! The doctors wrote of their commitment to change the way they practiced. They shared how they were impacted by our stories and the information provided.

After the presentation a jaw-dropping moment happened where time stood still and I was given a precious *gift*...

I was standing talking with four physicians who were congratulating us on what they considered an excellent presentation, when one of my doctors walked up to me and said the most powerful words. As she wept and wiped tears with her shirtsleeve, she said, "I failed you and I failed Grace. I am so sorry. I hope you will find it in your heart to forgive me. I will change the way I practice medicine because of Grace and because of what I have learned here today. I will not ignore the requests of my patients for additional monitoring and care. I will offer all I can to ensure the best possible outcome to my patients. Thank you for what you are doing!"

I tried to keep a professional composure, but the tears could not be contained. They spurted out of my eyes as I hugged the doctor. "That truly means the world to me. If I can help save even one life . . . Grace's death will not be in vain. Thank you for being willing to say what you said." In that moment, I felt the power of her words reach my soul. It felt like a healing balm had been applied to my heart. I was confident that *Grace's legacy assuredly included saving lives.*

Not long after the virtual doors to our organization's website were open, I was replying to over a hundred emails and calls a week from around the world. There were many twelve-hour days I was glued to my chair and computer responding and research- ing. I read every medical journal, peer-reviewed article, lecture, and website I could find that contained research on the topics of stillbirth, miscarriage, infant mortality, and grief. *My love of reading and research is another gift from Grace.*

I was a sponge soaking up copious amounts of information, which I managed to squeeze out and make it accessible, palatable, and useful to others. Our organization's website became the con- duit that ultimately yielded remarkable dividends in lives saved. Evidence came in calls, emails, and handwritten letters. *This golden example is one of the most redemptive gifts for me and a legacy for Grace.*

"Thank you so much! I am crying tears of joy as I write this. The education you provided to me about how to do baby move- ment monitoring (i.e., kick counts), and to be willing to advocate for my baby by being proactive in their care, helped save my baby's life. I was sent home after a doctor's appointment and was told I was fine, but I knew something wasn't right and I went back. I remained strong and determined in my requests to have my baby looked at as you suggested. Not long after, I received an emergency C-section due to the staff finally realizing my baby truly was in distress. Thank God my baby is alive and well! Thank you for what you are doing to educate and raise awareness. It saved my baby's life. I am forever grateful."

As I came across a need, a crack, or a hole on my path in the grief world, I went into my acts of service mode to address it. How can I help? What can I do? This was the impetus for so many of our programs and services we ended up offering through our organization over the years. The unknown and unintended by-product was the healing of hearts, mine included. We were growing faster than I could have ever imagined. It was time to leave my home cocoon and spread my wings anew. The need for additional measures of support continually was knocking on our door. No longer could we bear the weight of the demands on our own. We ventured out to recruit and train more volunteers to help.

Until this point, we found that hospitals commonly did not have a consistent packaged resource they could give the grieving mother. When a baby died, the mom might be given a small blanket or a baby outfit but some did not get one. Some received a grief book or a teddy bear and some did not. It all depended on what had been donated to the hospital or what was on hand at the moment in their storage room closet. We developed comforting and educational grief resources to give to parents. We package them in a GRACE Care Basket and a GRACE Care Tote Bag. They are ordered in advance by the hospital so the staff can provide a consistent resource for parents experiencing a miscarriage, still-birth, or neonatal loss. The contents help them create healing memories. Each one includes handmade items that volunteers sew, knit, and craft. Often they do so in memory of their own loved ones, so we attach their memorial note with those baskets and totes. Paying close attention to the delicate details, the volunteers make the baby clothing, blanket, GRACE Comfort Warmer, bracelet, and candle. Additionally, there is a teddy bear, a hand and foot molding kit, hair clipping packet, journal, pen, Missing GRACE literature, and books. The contents aid parents so they can grieve without regrets and affords them memories they will always treasure.

I began serving at local hospitals as a patient advocate for parents experiencing a perinatal loss, and soon requests came from far and wide to assist more families. The demands led me to recruit and train volunteers to assist in facilitating the bereavement care program I had developed, called the GRACE Crisis Care Team. Our team was on call 24/7 for hospitals and provided photography and videography, patient advocacy, birth support, and memorial service planning.

It was an incredible honor to serve each family. Every baby was a precious gift. I treasure in my heart the blessing of meeting and caring for each one. Grace's legacy is woven into each story as I was able to console and provide insight to the parents and their relatives who had questions and concerns. Parents became aware and informed of their rights, and the significance of their baby's life was validated before their eyes. I had a covert mission to shift the atmosphere from fear and panic to love and peace through quiet internal prayers and by being present fully with love for each person in the room. It was a delight to see parents move into a sense of empowerment by choosing to hold, photo-graph, and create healing memories with their babies.

The GRACE Crisis Care program was offered for ten years, at which time I transitioned to training hospital staff in how to provide the services internally in the Labor and Delivery, NICU, and Emergency Room Units.

When tragedy strikes and there is a death, people do not know instinctively what is helpful or hurtful or what will bring healing memories. Affected by the shock and intensity of emo- tions, they will gravitate to what feels safe and easier and avoid things that have any stigma or fear attached to it. It is critical to have guides with knowledge of what is helpful (the staff, friends, loved ones, or outside help) to explain the options for what we know now will be helpful postdelivery and beyond. Once upon a time, it was thought that parents were far better off to never see, hold, or spend any time with their baby if they died. Hospitals whisked the baby away and mothers were told it was for the best and to go on with their lives and try for another. We know now that these practices were harmful and caused parents to suppress their grief (remember Marge and Fred?). They were haunted by the absence of healing memories. I was grateful that there was a nurse in my hospital who made sure we received photos and had time to hold our baby. She was a voice for policy change in that hospital. It took years to institute that change but we benefited and are so appreciative.

"THIS IS NOT ACCEPTABLE!"

One day I opened a surprise document with words that felt like an explosive blast in my heart. It was my daughter's death certif-icate. Though it was obvious why I had it, I had never thought about receiving one. But there was just one piece of paper. Where was her birth certificate? There had to be a birth certificate too, right? I went through twenty-four hours of labor and delivered my baby. She was most certainly BORN! Maybe it was sent separately for some reason? I called the Minnesota Department of Health, expecting it was possibly just an oversight.

"Hello, I received my baby's death certificate today. My daughter Grace was stillborn and her birth certificate was not included. Can you please send me that document?"

"Ma'am, I am sorry but you don't get one. Your baby is only recognized by the state as DEAD and it's simply a document showing it died. We don't give out birth certificates for stillborn babies." There was a long, painful silence, and then I stammered, "But—she WAS BORN! I gave birth to her! How can she be acknowledged as . . . DEAD without ever being acknowledged as BORN?"

"Ma'am, that is just the way it is," she said, most matter-of-factly. "It's how it's set up by our government and frankly, just the way it's gonna have to be. Good luck ever changing it." My hand gripped the phone tighter and my other hand pressed against the gaping wound of my heart as if I was putting pressure on my chest so I wouldn't bleed out of the open wound. I took a deep breath and with an angry but quivering voice I said aloud, "I will change it! This is not acceptable!" I slammed down the phone with my trembling hand. "What in the world! How did this policy make sense in anyone's mind?"

I went into research mode for how to change what I felt was a detrimental policy. I was relieved to find another organization that had started paving a path for changing the laws to allow for parents like me to receive a birth certificate after having had a stillborn baby. My next move was to venture to the capitol in St. Paul, Minnesota, with a mission to help parents of a stillborn receive their baby's birth certificate. I rallied other stillbirth parents and guided them in how to write letters to their representatives. I was able to find committed senators and representatives to author and coauthor our bills. It took a few years, but eventually our bill received incredible legislative support on the floor of both the House and Senate and the health committee. The bill was signed into law and enacted August 1, 2005. I was standing next to our governor as he signed, handed me the pen, and shook my hand. As the press cameras clicked away *I looked up and thanked Grace for the gift of this monumental change and the strength to persevere to bring it to fruition.* I felt such gratitude for this *legacy* for Grace. Parents have shared through the years that receiving their birth certificates brought rightful recognition and dignity for their baby and tremendous peace and comfort to their hearts.

GRIEVING TOGETHER, LOVING TOGETHER

When bereaved parents have the opportunity to connect on a deeper level, good things happen. We started a grief support group out of our house. As the group grew in size we transitioned to a local church. It quickly became apparent that the couples who attended the group fared far better in their marriage when active in the group. The couples would confer with having similar struggles in their relationships, which was validating for them. We began sharing about the five love languages to help address these struggles. We had members take the quiz to discover their love languages, which proved insightful. Laughter between couples lightened the emotional climate as they learned why each person had been loving their mate the way they did. Couples reflected on their prior trials and shared personal stories of how they had missed the mark in trying to love each other. Little by little they grew in understanding how to effectively touch their mate's heart and love them well. *It was as if they had found a mystery key that led them to find a secret door that opened up a room full of treasures in the house they thought they had known so well.* It was adventurous and exciting to try new ways of loving each other and even more pleasing to see positive results for their efforts. Shortly after going through the book and putting the principles into effect, we were hearing encouraging feedback from husbands and wives that they were feeling much closer than before and communication had improved, which was helping them grieve together. It didn't mean everything was roses all of a sudden, but tangible hope and effective tools were keeping the marriage boat afloat. They expressed feeling more assured of their love and commitment to each other.

Emerging themes and initiatives arose from our online groups and in-person meetings. The people attending our support groups often drove over an hour to attend. They felt there was an overall lack of grief support, resources, and awareness in their communities, hospitals, clinics, and churches. This compelled us to ask the questions, "Might we be able to provide even more comprehensive support? Could we inspire others to do more to help as well?" Ultimately, we discovered that yes, we could. We formed together and defined a new mission that embodied the love we have for our daughter and for the people who had become our friends through grieving. We realized there was a way for us to help more families on a much grander scale. Our smaller, mom-and-pop Missing GRACE organization became a 501(c)(3) nonprofit foundation.

This is a *legacy* for Grace. GRACE is an acronym with a meaning central to the heart of the foundation's mission:

1. **Grieve** in healthy ways by giving comfort, support, and resources

2. **Restore** holistically in emotional, relational, physical, and spiritual health

3. **Arise** from the ashes—the dark place of deep sorrow—and discover there is hope for a brighter day

4. **Commemorate** loved ones—honor them

5. **Educate** by sharing your own story of loss and help to save lives

www.missingGRACE.org

"TWO IN HEAVEN, TWO ON EARTH"

Our foundation grew by leaps and bounds, and we soon were helping thousands of people. That felt really good, but it didn't magically remove or fill the place of longing for a baby of our own that we could raise. With Grace we got pregnant right away; now the months of trying turned to years of infertility. There were three empty rooms in our big house, waiting. As I walked past them each day on my way to my desk, I envisioned our future children's names in pretty framed signs next to the door of their room. Adoption would have been a wonderful way to grow our family; however, we had two failed domestic adoptions. We then went the route of the foster system to foster-adopt, but discovered it wasn't available in the county where we resided.

As we went through these situations, we grieved anew for each loss. We met many other bereaved parents who were dealing with infertility and adoption challenges as well. The repeated and ongoing grief of infertility and failed adoptions on top of previous pregnancy loss was an even more silent grief than still-birth. Like us, these parents felt such embarrassment, shame, and hopelessness. The struggle was REAL. Unraveling the mess of compounded grief and layers of loss from this Pandora's box was mind-boggling. We could not find any place that offered specific support for these combined issues. We did more research and net-worked and ultimately connected with many professionals who could provide applicable infertility and adoption services for us personally and for the families we served.

The cause of our infertility was finally discovered and was addressed. A month later we conceived our second baby! What joyous and terrifying news! We were so elated to be pregnant, but it was scary knowing full well all the risks and concerns. Our first rainbow baby required two months of bed rest after hemorrhaging and then four more months in bed after going into labor at twenty weeks. I was put on medications to stop labor. Me, lying in a bed on my left side, while running our foundation from my sideways laptop and phone on speaker was truly one of the more challeng-ing seasons of my life. I was a wreck emotionally. It was painful on so many levels, but I had high hopes that I would come home with a baby. Home fetal-monitoring was not only comforting but proved lifesaving. It was confirmed that our second baby had um-bilical cord entanglement. "Oh dear God . . . not again!" I thought as my heart beat outside my chest. I would have been undone at that terrifying news had I not had so much support in place. It was no easy task to stay calm and at peace in the face of so many chal-lenges. Stints in the hospital were necessary for additional testing when fetal movement slowed and home fetal heart rate recordings didn't look normal. It was a tremendous relief to have attentive and proactive care from Dr. Collins. He delivered our first rainbow daughter via emergency C-section due to fetal stress at thirty-five weeks, and she spent ten days in the NICU in Louisiana.

Three and a half years later, to our delight, came another rainbow baby. Our third daughter, who also had a double-nuchal cord, was born healthy at thirty-six weeks gestation and came home without any NICU time and less drama. The whole birth and recovery actually went rather smoothly and was even quite pleasant.

Our fourth baby—a surprise, miracle pregnancy—was never to be held this side of heaven. Our baby miscarried at fifteen weeks gestation. We named the baby Promise, with the expectation of a promise fulfilled when we meet our baby in heaven. When asked how many children we have, I often reply, "We have two in heaven and two on earth."

Both our living children look similar to each other and to Grace. I see her in them, and that is most definitely a precious *gift*. They are both very inclusive of Grace and Promise and speak of their siblings often, sharing their story when given the opportunity. Their family drawings include Grace and Promise. This blesses my heart. They are very sensitive and considerate about the plight of bereaved families. They love participating in and helping with all our foundation's events too! Running our organization is a family affair.

One event we really enjoy together is our annual memorial run/walk. The first one, called Kaila & Grace's Hope & Hearts Run, was held September 2006 and it has been held every fall since. The event includes a 5K run, memorial walk, kids' fun dash, and a remembrance ceremony. These events raise awareness about pregnancy loss and stillbirth prevention. Now it's called the Minnesota Hope & Hearts Run/Walk. Bereaved families from all over

Minnesota and the Midwest participate. Hope & Hearts events have been held in Texas, New Mexico, Kentucky, and Ohio.

My heart was so full and so were my arms. I was juggling parenting a four-year-old and nursing a baby while running our foundation out of our home. It was a beautiful yet crazy life. My assistant mentioned the elephant in the room and said, chuckling, "Your house has been overtaken by all the baskets and you are bursting at the seams here! Your organization has grown to the point you need a separate space outside of your home. You also need more help!"

So we began the transition. Our dream was to create a safe place where bereaved parents, their families, and care providers in the community could access timely resources and grief support services all under one roof. The vision for the special gathering place would include a library, counseling services, support groups, classes, a gift shop with unique memorial items, community meeting rooms, and plenty of space to store, assemble, and ship our basket, tote, and literature resources.

In June 2011, thanks to a tremendous outpouring of support by the community, our vision became a reality when we opened the Center for GRACE, which has become a place of hope and healing in Minnesota for families grieving the loss of a baby or child. When people have a bad day, want to connect with others on a similar journey, or are ready to serve and give back in memory of their child, the Center for GRACE is available. The facility also serves as the headquarters for the foundation and volunteers offer phone and online support as well. Ultimately, it's a conduit for healing.

Healing in the grief journey is so multidimensional. It takes us by surprise because it doesn't usually look the way we imagined it

> The key was looking outside of our own pain.

would. One day, you realize that things that once hurt you before don't hurt now. Things that were difficult are easier now. You can admit there are blessings that have emerged from those dark seasons of your grief.

As we poured ourselves into the foundation, there was an unexpected benefit for our labor of love: a path to new layers of healing. The key was looking outside of our own pain, while being transparent about what we felt as we came alongside others to support them through their pain. In grieving, it is natural to turn inward for a time. However, if we keep that focus, opportunities pass us by that can open doors to healing in our lives. It's not easy to open up to others when sorrowing, but there is a great reward and blessing if you do.

I have been asked, "If you knew what you know now, would you do it all over again and go through the loss of Grace?" In the beginning I might have been tempted to say, no, because all I wanted was my baby. I replayed the ways I could somehow have her back. I longed, wished, prayed, and hoped for something that was not within my reach. My brain wanted to escape to a fairy tale that could turn back time. More than anything, I wished I could have Grace in my life here on earth. But once I stopped the daydreaming and my mind returned to reality, I couldn't entertain those thoughts anymore. It was not the way life had played out for us. I finally accepted that bad things happen to good people in this life. It's not because I was so terrible and deserved that bad thing. Not because of anything we could point to—it just happened. To change our story to having Grace alive in my life . . . it would cause a ripple effect more than my mind can grasp. Would I have my other two precious children in my life? Would I be who I am today with the same knowledge, insight, empathy, and faith? I can surmise that I would not, and much of the story that I love and appreciate would have changed. I am at peace. *I have been given many gifts from Grace. I anticipate I will receive more gifts along the way as I embrace the ongoing mission to carry on her legacy.*

YOUR TURN

Can you smile through the tears? Have you discovered it's possible to grieve with hope? If you are still deep in your grief and the future looks bleak, hang on! Hold tight to hope! There is a beautiful life for your child after their death, and there is a beautiful life for us who still remain. Choose to persevere and you will discover the many gifts awaiting you along the journey!

1. What was most helpful for you from this chapter?

2. What gifts have you received in this grief journey so far?

3. Have you missed some of the gifts that were too hard to accept at the time but maybe now you can receive, open, and enjoy?

4. What gifts have you been able to give away because of your loved one's story?

5. Do you wish for your loved one to have a legacy?

6. What legacy would you like to create for them?

7. What legacy do you think they would have wanted?

8. What steps can you take to begin building the legacy?

9. Do you need to rally support from others to make this possible?

10. Who could you invite to help make this happen with you?

Afterword

OUR GUESS IS THAT if you have read this book you have done so with tears, rooted in the pain of your own loss or that of a family member or friend. That loss may have occurred many years ago, or much more recently. Either way, reflecting on the death of a child always brings pain, and pain is often accompanied by tears. However, we know that crying is a healthy way to process grief. So the tears you may have experienced as you have read are not wasted. Rather, they are helping you continue the journey of grieving your loss.

We hope that you have identified with many of the true stories of others who have walked this road. We also hope that you have been motivated to share your journey with others. Too often we think that others are not interested in where we are emotionally, because they don't ask questions. However, many friends and family mistakenly think that to bring up the topic of your loss will upset you. Therefore, you must take the initiative to talk about your present state in processing your grief. If you introduce the topic, friends will usually listen empathetically and often ask questions. Talking about the details of what happened and how you felt then and now is one of the most helpful means of processing your grief.

As you walk the road of grief, your need for love has not diminished. If you are married, the person you would most like to love you is your spouse. If your "love tank" is full, and you feel secure in the love of your spouse, your loss is much easier to process. If you do not feel loved by your spouse, you may experience even greater isolation. We hope that by now you have discovered each other's primary love language and are speaking it regularly.

As we have discussed, husbands and wives often process their grief in very different ways. If we are not aware of this, we can misinterpret the behavior of our spouse. It is our desire that this section of the book will bring communication and understanding so that the two of you can walk together through your loss. Speaking each other's love language creates a positive emotional climate, which makes it easier to talk about our differences and thus enhance understanding.

This book may also help friends and family who have not experienced the loss of a baby to better understand the normal process of grief. Hopefully they will learn how to be more helpful by avoiding hurtful statements, and speaking words of comfort and understanding. If they understand the concept of the five love languages and know your primary love language, they too can be more effective in communicating their love.

More churches, organizations, and healthcare professionals are coming to recognize the need for support groups for those who have lost a child. The grief journey is easier when we walk with others who can relate from experience. We believe this book will serve as a resource for such a group. Reading a chapter and then sharing your thoughts and feelings with the group provides a forum for meaningful dialogue.

If perhaps you are not located in close proximity to a support group, Missing GRACE Foundation offers online support groups that can be accessed from anywhere. There are a wide variety of online chat groups and support forums that can be found with a web search as well.

It is our prayer that this book will serve as a welcome companion as you walk the unexpected pathway of grief. We hope it is one of your valued tools to help you grieve in healthy ways and you will experience sustained healing.

— GARY CHAPMAN

Acknowledgments

EACH OF THE STORIES within these pages carries great significance. Each has touched my (Candy's) life. Thank you to all the individuals who have had the courage to share their heart, their hurt, and their tears. Your perseverance and love for your babies is inspiring. I am honored to have seen, held, photographed, and spent time with your babies. To honor your privacy, we have not used any of your real names. To the babies and children in heaven that were mentioned and represented in this book, you are never forgotten and you hold a special place in my heart. Your stories live on and continue to touch so many lives and now hopefully even more.

Gary and Candy offer a special thanks to Karolyn Chapman and Anita Hall, the wonderful ladies who edited the manuscript with such care. You were both so helpful to offer encouragement just when it was needed most in this process. We are truly so grateful to work with such a remarkable team at Northfield Publishing. Thank you, John Hinkley, Betsey Newenhuyse, and the folks who were behind the scenes bringing all the pieces together.

Marie Larson, your prayers and input were so timely in getting me (Candy) through the "stuck" moments.

To my two babies (not so small anymore) whom I hold in my arms as often as they let me. Tatum and Talyah, you are such blessings. I marvel that God gave me the both of you. I love you both dearly. Thank you for your patience and understanding with the time needed to write this book. To answer your question, "Are you done yet, Mom?" Yes, I am! I finished the book!

To my best friend, father of my babies and life's partner, your love has made all the difference. Stephen, your gift of encouragement and believing in me throughout this process has kept me going. Thank you for your insight and guidance with the manuscript, for all the times you took care of our home and children so I could be writing. You have sacrificed so much for me and for our family. God has used you to show me the depth of His love for His bride.

Abba Father, You have never left me, never forsaken me. You have been there to hold me so tenderly, wiped away my tears and given me joy in exchange for my sorrow. I know You have good plans and I trust You. I give this to You as an offering.

Notes

Chapter 1: When Your World Comes Crashing Down

1. Merriam-Webster's, s.v. "survive," https://www.merriam-webster.com/dictionary/survive.
2. English-Word Information, s.v. "survivor," https://wordinfo.info/unit/2318/page:4.
3. Psalm 30:5 (NKJV).

Chapter 2: Grieving the Loss of a Baby You Never Knew

1. Guttmacher Institute, Fact Sheet, "Induced Abortion in the United States," September 2019, https://www.guttmacher.org/fact-sheet/induced-abortion-united-states.
2. Guttmacher Institute, Fact Sheet, "Global Incidence and Trends," March 2018, https://www.guttmacher.org/fact-sheet/induced-abortion-worldwide.
3. John 14:27 (ESV)
4. EMDR Institute Inc., https://www.emdr.com.
5. Brainspotting, https://brainspotting.com.
6. "Sand Tray Therapy," GoodTherapy, last updated August 6, 2019, https://www.goodtherapy.org/learn-about-therapy/types/sand-tray-sand-play-therapy.
7. American Art Therapy Association, https://arttherapy.org.
8. American Music Therapy Association, https://www.musictherapy.org.

9. Good Therapy, Equine-Assisted Therapy, https://www.goodtherapy .org/learn-about-therapy/types/equine-assisted-therapy.
10. First Thessalonians 4:13 (ESV).

Chapter 3: Our Journey

1. Create a log of your baby's movements or use a kick count app. Monitor at a similar time each night once you are twenty-eight weeks gestation. Document how many movements you count in an hour. Ideally, you should detect an average of ten definite movements in two hours. Babies sleep, and there may be times in the day when you feel little or no movement. If you do not detect ten movements after two hours, go in to Labor and Delivery to receive an NST (Non-Stress Test) where they can monitor your baby's heartbeat, movements, and detect if you are having any contractions.
2. Case Report in Obstetrics and Gynecology. 2012; 2012: 308206, doi: 10.1155/2012/308206, PMCID: PMC3517836, PMID: 23243528, Velamentous Cord Insertion in a Singleton Pregnancy: An Obscure Cause of Emergency Cesarean—A Case Report, "Velamentous cord insertion (VCI) is an abnormal cord insertion (CI) in which the umbilical vessels diverge as they traverse between the amnion and chorion before reaching the placenta. Because of the lack of protection from Wharton's jelly, these vessels are prone to compression and rupture," November 29, 2012, https://www.ncbi.nlm.nih.gov/pmc/ articles/PMC3517836.

Chapter 4: Loving Your Mate Well in the Midst of Grief

1. Proverbs 18:21 (ESV).

Chapter 5: For Friends of the Grieving: How You Can Help—and Hurt

1. Adapted from "Helpful and Hurtful Things People Say and Do," GRACE Resource Folder, Missing GRACE Foundation.

Chapter 8: These Shoes Don't Fit, but You Can't Take Them Off

1. Psalm 23:4 (ESV).

LOVE + HOPE SERIES

The 5 Love Languages® for Life's Complex Circumstances

FINDING STRENGTH, GAINING COURAGE, AND LOVING WELL

KEEPING LOVE ALIVE AS MEMORIES FADE

The 5 Love Languages® and the Alzheimer's Journey

Deborah Barr, MA • Edward G. Shaw, MD

GARY CHAPMAN, PhD

978-0-8024-1450-2

BUILDING LOVE TOGETHER IN BLENDED FAMILIES

The 5 Love Languages® and Becoming Stepfamily Smart

GARY CHAPMAN, PhD
and RON L. DEAL, MMFT

978-0-8024-1905-7

SHARING LOVE ABUNDANTLY IN SPECIAL NEEDS FAMILIES

The 5 Love Languages® for Parents Raising Children with Disabilities

GARY CHAPMAN, PhD
and Jolene Philo, MEd

978-0-8024-1862-3

also available as eBooks and audiobooks

NORTHFIELD
PUBLISHING

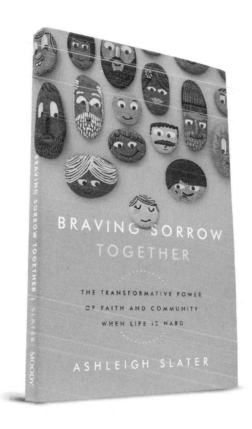